People Magnet

How to Be the Most Extraordinary Person

(The Ultimate Guide to Learn How to Interact and Communicate Effectively)

Steven Tillman

Published By **Kate Sanders**

Steven Tillman

All Rights Reserved

People Magnet: How to Be the Most Extraordinary Person (The Ultimate Guide to Learn How to Interact and Communicate Effectively)

ISBN 978-1-7782615-2-7

No part of this guidebook shall be reproduced in any form without permission in writing from the publisher except in the case of brief quotations embodied in critical articles or reviews.

Legal & Disclaimer

The information contained in this book is not designed to replace or take the place of any form of medicine or professional medical advice. The information in this book has been provided for educational & entertainment purposes only.

The information contained in this book has been compiled from sources deemed reliable, and it is accurate to the best of the Author's knowledge; however, the Author cannot guarantee its accuracy and validity and cannot be held liable for any errors or omissions. Changes are periodically made to this book. You must consult your doctor or get professional medical advice before using any of the suggested remedies, techniques, or information in this book.

Upon using the information contained in this book, you agree to hold harmless the Author from and against any damages, costs, and expenses, including any legal fees potentially resulting from the application of any of the information provided by this guide. This disclaimer applies to any damages or injury caused by the use and application, whether directly or indirectly, of any advice or information presented, whether for breach of contract, tort, negligence, personal injury, criminal intent, or under any other cause of action.

You agree to accept all risks of using the information presented inside this book. You need to consult a professional medical practitioner in order to ensure you are both able and healthy enough to participate in this program.

Table Of Contents

Chapter 1: What Can You Do To Attract People 1

Chapter 2: Feel Important To Them 17

Chapter 3: We Agree With Other Those. 28

Chapter 4: Communicate Effectively 33

Chapter 5: Make Yourself an Influencer . 52

Chapter 6: How Do You Convince People To Be Real Quickly? 66

Chapter 7: Listen To the Views of Other People 87

Chapter 8: The Psychology of Likeability 101

Chapter 9: Developing Charisma 111

Chapter 10: Building Strong Connections 122

Chapter 11: Networking Strategies 131

Chapter 12: Overcoming Social Anxiety 140

Chapter 13: Navigating Difficult Relationships 150

Chapter 14: Highlight Your Alluring Characteristics 159

Chapter 15: Secret 167

Chapter 16: Want............................... 173

Chapter 17: Consider Your Fellowships a Speculation 180

Chapter 1: What Can You Do To Attract People

We looked over Dale Carnegie's tips for being an effective listener, and on making others talk about themselves. I suggested a few simple questions that could be used as discussions starting points. These were simply icebreaker questions intended to break the ice and have fun. In this week's lesson, we'll look at some ideas which complement our previous lessons for example, the best way to frame conversations with regard to your partner's needs.

Then you came out and expressed interest in the discussion. It is possible that you will find points of common interest and with this individual. When you discover that people share common interests, it's more easy to communicate with each other and build lasting relationships. According to the notion of liking, we're more likely to enjoy a relationship with people who share our interests.

As an example, my hobbies include fitness as well as martial arts and business. Conversations can continue for hours, in the event that I get to know somebody who is passionate in one of these areas. What happens if I meet people who do not have the same passions as us?

Imagine you have a conversation with someone who immediately tells you that they enjoy dangerous actions. What do you do even if you think there is nothing you share? The only thing you need do is discuss extreme sports. It's simple.

Be interested, be sure to ask lots of questions, and then take this as a chance to gain knowledge. It's been a long time since I've thought about on a bungee jump," you could begin. What was the reason that enticed you to make that leap there's certainly an interesting and touching story behind the initial leap. The rush of adrenaline from that first jump is bound to come back when one remembers the events leading to the jump, as well as the leap itself. There are a variety of motives why this is great opportunity for you.

In the beginning, they'll begin to accuse you of the way they feel. We can safely assume that everybody appreciates a positive mood from time to time. People naturally are drawn to and eager to be with you when they enjoy having you around. An excellent way to begin an association.

A second reason is that having a link to these emotions can make the person you are speaking to be noticed. It's a good thing because it boosts the chance of someone remembering the person you're with and what you've spoken about. Are you aware of someone you knew but chose to not engage in conversation due to the fact that you weren't confident enough to inquire about the name of the person to ask them again? It is easier to remember your name, which reduces possibility that someone will decide to stay away from you since they aren't able to remember your name.

It's easy to structure your thoughts around the interests of your opponent. All you need is to be willing to learn and be patient enough to ask thoughtful questions. Many people find it difficult to stay open and patient.

We're always looking for public recognition. If someone talks to us and doesn't give us the chance to reply, we become uneasy. A person who doesn't trust you enough to risk in a relationship not the type of person you would like to have to have in your life. Be aware that building a business is not the goal if you are in a professional partnership.

There's a major deficiency of listening abilities in our society. A majority of people who listen are not listening in the hope of understanding what's being said, instead, they are listening to be able by adding their own thoughts. It's been difficult for a long time to listen with a keen eye however, with the plethora of modern distractions, it's harder nowadays.

Conversations can be fun if you have a good listening ability and formulate your answers according to what interests the other person has. It allows you to learn more about the person you are talking to and enhances the chance that you'll learn valuable knowledge. This week, I'm challenging you to shift your focus towards other people, and then to engage with people by engaging in ways that matter for the other. It will be easier to gain allies and influence more people to join if you take this approach.

Being more interested and genuinely in different people is an effective method to enhance your interpersonal skills. It will enable you to easily connect with people who you would like to make acquaintances with. Some people do not have the motivation or desire to explore what's happening around them. While they might not look for it, some people are happy to hear what they are exposed to. This article is written specifically for those who fall in this class.

To build genuine friendships, you must train yourself to be interested in the lives of others, their thoughts, and dreams. If you need any help you need, here are 17 suggestions to share with you. If you follow these principles, you'll begin to develop an interest for the world of those who are around you.

Recognize the importance of narratives

The realization that each person's unique story could help you become more attentive to others. Find something valuable from the stories of others. It is important to try and find these stories. By reading a single story it will give you so much more understanding and insight.

Telling a story can provide a glimpse to the past, brain, and the hopes of another. The ability to see into their lives can be a wonderful way to gain insight into the past, mind and aspirations of another. Be sure to keep these tips at the forefront when you are interacting with others. Make sure you are listening to what stories they're likely to share with to you.

Consider what is preventing your curiosity about others and work on it.

If you're experiencing difficulty expressing interest to the other individuals, take a look about the reason. Do you think there is no point to communicate with people for you? Think you're aware of everything you need to know regarding this subject? Perhaps you've tried to show concern for others previously, but didn't make solid friendships.

Discover where the problem originates, no matter what it could be. It will be easier to identify the issue, and this will motivate you to act and make an improvement. Also, be aware that the current will always be different from the previous.

Empathize

Put your self in the position someone else is a great method to demonstrate that you are concerned about the person. Consider the issue from an outsider's viewpoint. Be aware of the emotions associated with the words they're using. If they appear to be upset this moment, try to show compassion. Let them share their joy If you are able to.

Empathy is an incredibly powerful talent. One of its many advantages is the fact that it can assist you in becoming more engaged in people who are around you. Make use of this tool to be emotionally effective to interact with other people.

Widen your perspective.

A wider view can help you connect to people. If you're a person who is open You won't be able to let the fact that some people aren't as enthused about their views you. Most likely, you'll be happy with your new perspective. People's desire to be involved in discussion with those with different opinions is increased as their tolerance increases.

In the event that, on average 50% of the people whom you meet differ from yours, this could be very beneficial. Maintain an open mind, and you'll have no problem when you get to know many people.

The focus should be on the global in general and also oneself.

If a desire to know more about others on its own doesn't suffice to inspire your interest, you'd like to do something a bit more ambitious. Concentrate on the entire world instead of focusing on the individual. Examine the environment around your current life. Discover the history of its history, its diverse traditions, and most important, its inhabitants.

It will allow you to create a curiosity that is natural. In the end, when it reaches into your interactions it's impossible not to be curious about every aspect of your life. It is essential to learn all you can about your friends and acquaintances.

Find out more on the subject.

If you're even showing an interest in the world around you, it's time to start educating yourself by studying the subjects that interest you. Read! The book is likely to have been written in the topic(s) you're interested in.

The best way to increase your cognition capabilities by increasing the amount you read. According to some, reading to the mind is the same as sharpening a sword to a blade. You'll be eager to find out more about everything will grow when your IQ grows. Your curiosity will increase about individuals.

Try to maintain your expectations in check.

Although it's essential to possess an open mind and explore education and gain experience in order to gain a better understanding of others' viewpoints, it's equally important to be realistic about your expectations. It's easy to be enthralled about the utterances of someone else. The excitement level will increase to dangerous levels. It is possible that you will be disappointed by their stories when they share them with you.

It is therefore important to be realistic about your expectations. Certain stories don't live with your expectation. They aren't as idealistic, and more connected to real life and author's personal experience. Remember that these stories also possess value and are beautiful. If you're insisting that each story be amazing and exhilarating it's likely that you'll be deceived from time the next.

Another possibility is that the person you're speaking to simply doesn't want to speak the conversation to you. In the end they may be among one of the least sociable person you've ever met. That's perfectly fine too. They may have monsters to take down. Give them a bit of privacy.

Don't forget to take mental notes, and then seek clarification.

For a greater get the most benefit out of your interactions with your friends It could be beneficial to keep a notepad handy while you're talking. You may gain a few nuggets of wisdom from whatever topic people are talking about. At times it is common for them to make a comment which provides a bit of details about themselves. Each of these are crucial information to keep in mind.

If you were having a chat about vacations that have passed, someone can talk about a specific beach and the incredible surfing there is. It is easy to tell that they enjoy the surf and beach when they share an account like this. It is possible to make an outline of the story and then follow it up with a series of additional questions.

Be able to continue conversations

If you want to become more in touch with others It will assist you become a better communication expert. The ability you have to start and keep a conversation going will affect the extent to which you can get meet someone else.

If you're not naturally attracted, increasing the skills of communication will increase your willingness to the possibility of new adventures. There will be two different forms of social competence concurrently.

The art of conversation is far too intricate to discuss on its own. If you're seeking some more tips to improve your skills in conversation This site offers more information about where it came from.

Be aware of the efforts you can make to show an interest in others an aspect of your professional growth.

The process of identifying ways to show greater interest in others is an enjoyable and stimulating activity. So, think of this as an opportunity to learn. Transform this experience into an educational possibility of epic proportions.

Take this test as a way to prepare before you decide to be serious about your work. Find as much info as you can from this article before putting it on the line in real life. Yes, it is possible to think like students and gain knowledge. This experience alone will make you more intrigued by other people that will benefit your well in the years to come.

Reduce your introspection.

It is important to stop being so focused on yourself when you wish to think about others. Instead of being focused on your own self, focus on the other person. Concentrate on them like they were the only important aspect. So, you'll listen to their words in their totality and become curious about the other individuals you meet.

People you are familiar with will spark your interest.

Doing this is among the many ways to make your life easier. Meet people you think that you'll enjoy being around instead of those might be interesting.

Consider the scenario of locating people you know that participate in an activity, or who is working in an area you're little about, but you are curious about. Take the initiative to begin an exchange with them. Befriend them with ease. Take the time to find out more about them.

As you practice this and the more you do it, the less awkward be when you meet people and strike off conversations. This is more likely to come naturally to you when you meet people that whom you admire, but when you've mastered it eventually, you'll be able employ the same strategy for all.

Meet other people that are interested in the same interests as you.

As it is easy to feel a connection with people with similar interests to yours and interests, it's easy to create feelings about those you admire. Even even if you're a pro on your subject It's fascinating to learn about the viewpoint of someone else about the topic.

Therefore, it is suggested that you seek out individuals who have similar passions. Connect with people around you who are interested in subjects that are important to each of you. Find a community with a similar interest or better yet to create your own. This way, you can explore this idea with strangers you've not had the pleasure of meeting before, and discover people who have the same interests as you.

Be sure to pay attention to more subtle clues.

If you're hoping to feel more concerned about others, then you'll have to improve your ability to observe equally. As long as you're not engaged in a private and deep conversation with someone else, you need that you pay the attention of more than the individual or thing before you.

Chapter 2: Feel Important To Them

It's normal to want those you love to feel that they are special. It's good to know that there's various ways to do this that range from small gestures of kindness to frank gestures of love. If you require more tips on how you can help someone feel loved read on.

1. Make use of their first names.

Making someone feel unique by your gaze with this way. Being able to hear your name is satisfying for most people. And being addressed by their full name makes make them feel unique. If you're looking to create an impression, you should use the name of a person instead of only "hi" when you greet them. Begin or finish any sentence by mentioning their name, regardless of whether the topic is an inquiry or praise, or just a comment.

A phrase like "Hey Sam!" can be effective. We were delighted to see Louis at the conference today, Louis, and it was great seeing your face today.

2. They compliment each other.

If you are kind to someone they feel valued and special. Express your gratitude for their amazing vocals or for their skills at the kitchen. Thank them for all the qualities they have. Let them know that you value and appreciate the individual they are and that your effort to make use of their strengths were worth it.

You can try a flattery such as "You are a great cook!. In the last few weeks I've been thinking about the spaghetti you cooked.

3 Listen to the words they're using.

Recognizing and being appreciated is a crucial aspect of one's perception of self-worth. Take note of what someone says. Turn off the telephone and pay them complete focus while they're speaking. Make use of active listening strategies like paraphrasing what they've spoken.

If you'd like them to chat on Try smiling and nodding to them.

4 Ask them questions.

This shows that you value them more than the level of their appearance. Think about any questions you'd like to have answered in an appropriate check-in. Be sure to inquire about their wellbeing or any recent activity. Contact them about how their day is progressing.

You can ask them questions such as "What type of programs are you applying to?" as well as "Do you have a favorite program so far?" If they're submitting an application to graduate school.

The five most desirable traits of the team.

Feel special with a compliment on their abilities or their expertise. Ask your friend who is a musician the questions regarding certain instruments or about the past of music while you take in the day in an institution that is dedicated to this art. While giving them a sense of pride in their work, they could also learn something new while doing it.

Perhaps you or a friend who is a fan of DIY projects are currently undergoing the process of renovating. Get their input regarding the subject.

6. Send them a message for them to know that you're taking note of the possibility of them.

A simple text or note could make an influence. You can send them an SMS next time you experience an urge to recall this summer's great times. A reminder from someone else is an incredibly thoughtful gesture nearly everyone will appreciate. An opportunity to remind them of what they've accomplished in their lives can be a great incentive.

Write them a note with a message that says, "I was just thinking about how you and I spent at the beach with each other last year. It was a wonderful moment! I hope that everything goes well with you.

7 Give them the gift by gifting them a present or creating something unique.

The self-esteem of a person can increase when receiving an item of their choice. It's not necessary to shell out a large amount of money or overspend. In the event you come across you again, take an assortment of their most-loved chips and take them to. Choose a unique mug is sure to please them on the road.

Send them a gift which is personalised to their needs and interests for them to feel special. There's no better gift than the sketchbook, or even a drawing pencil set for someone who is fond of creating art with paper.

If you're an artist You can even make your own present. Cook them dinner If you're a skilled cook.

We've had the pleasure of feeling warm and gratefulness sincere. These moments made us feel better and encouraged us to perform better and do more.

There have been instances where we felt like that we'd be disregarded or dismissed. It's an experience that is all too familiar: You put in a lot of effort and adhere to the guidelines, but still being ignored. Maybe those words were in the mail however the innocuous "thanks" didn't come off as significant or serious.

This is not the type that you would want to surround yourself with while you try to convey gratitude! Beware of this trap, and express gratitude in a way that is meaningful will go a long way in making the day of someone else.

1. Definition of your terms.

In what way do you feel thankful? Who was responsible for that? Detailing your responses makes you appear more genuine. One of the keys in expressing gratitude is being specific.

Do not just use the phrase "Thanks for cleaning" if you have a partner who does extra tasks around the house. You can say something else in the form of "Thank you for folding all that clothes!" You put in an awful job to stay at the top of the line. That's why, "thank you."

The right response may not always be apparent. (Let's admit it, we all have there is a problem with verbal diarrhea.) This is why it may be beneficial to make a point of your daily routine to think about how people close to you have assisted in the past. Tell them how much you appreciate their help. It will have great value!

2. Define the assistance that they gave.

It's important to pay attention when praising someone, as the article suggests. In thinking about the person is important not to just mention specifics about what they've done but also what it did for you.

In the end as a result, you'll recognize the importance of the actions of their leaders.

Imagine making a gesture of appreciation in exchange for a gift. The simple phrase "Thank you for the money" isn't enough. Perhaps you can go on to say something like "Thank to you for this wonderful present. It was spent in a snorkeling excursion during our honeymoon. Thank you for your generosity that we could build memories that be cherished for a lifetime.

For example, if someone made notes during the last meeting, instead of thanking them for their work, instead of saying "thank you," explain the reason why their assistance has been important. In this case, for instance it is possible to say "I thank you for taking notes during our last meeting. In the following months, every person in the group has relied upon your notes to refresh their minds about the key points of the meeting. The team has been able to move forward much faster due to this. I'm hoping you'll understand that you're valued.

The third step is to add your personal note.

Encourage the other person as well as their strengths with a positive comment about their character. You can say, "I like how well you handle the details since that's not one of my skills."

Let me add a small observation: We're not trying to focus on ourselves however, consider the fact that praises can reveal something about the person giving them. The people who feel confident that they are worth it will be generous in their words of praise. Your happiness that you bring others by taking the time to acknowledge their good traits will boost your confidence.

Take your phone off in the event that you would like to show appreciation to anyone! Engage in discussion and maintain an eye contact person or person(s).Fourth be a surprise gesture of your gratitude.

Being greeted from the heart by someone who isn't your friend is appreciated by all. If someone isn't expecting that, you could make their day.

Make an effort to put smiles on the face of someone who you love that you've never acknowledged or perhaps isn't looking forward to hearing from you with this kind of gesture. It's possible to pick the phone and make an ex-colleague a phone call or take a former employer for lunch so that you can thank them for their contribution to the company.

If you want to demonstrate that you value your relationship by using the old practice of sending a letter in person. While you may be worried that this makes you appear old-fashioned, it actually makes people feel very loved. If someone doesn't do any specific thing to you, it's good to tell them that you value what they do by writing them an individual note of appreciation. gratitude.

It could be something like, "Hey, I know you volunteer at the shelter in your spare time and I just want to let you know I value that." Alternately: "You always have a smile on your face whenever you arrive at your job. I'm inspired by your example. The act of acknowledging someone in a surprising way can be lots of enjoyable.

5) Give them rewards.

If we're talking about "gift," we're not discussing an expensive new car or anything expensive. There's a possibility of putting a piece of stickers inside your children's lunch boxes, put an unopened cup of coffee on the desk of someone else, write a few notes of support on a post-it note and bake your spouse's most loved food, and so forth. Do something unique! It doesn't have to cost a lot.

Chapter 3: We Agree With Other Those

Have you ever wondered the best way to convey your approval with the words of someone else? In reality, there instances where simply saying "yes" would be inappropriate. There are a variety of situations that require you to affirm your agreement to someone else or offer some explanation.

There are a array of affirmatively worded as well as phrases in English.

For a quick and easy demonstration of that you are in agreement You could use the following examples:

Yeah, I believe this way.

Sure.

Absolutely!

Definitely.

Yes, me too.

Of course.

It's exactly how I feel as well.

This is how I feel.

So do I.

If you take a close look at two people conversing in English You'll notice that they often use the phrases "Sure," "surely," "absolutely," and "of course." These phrases let the person speaking be aware that you're curious about their conversation, and also encourage you to not stop with out getting out of the discussion.

"I agree, "I agree," "me too," "I also believe that," or "I also feel that," whenever you want to add more detail on what other person's opinion is or to add your own, is standard. If you're in agreement with another person, they may require you to explain the position you take.

They are essentially basic words however, you can additionally use a more sophisticated words to communicate your disagreement with anyone.

As an example:

Wow! You've put my thoughts in a perfect way.

There's no way to say my appreciation for the way you think.

It was a good point.

I am completely in approval on this point.

It is normal to have occasions when you need to suggest your appreciation for someone's viewpoint however, you still want to express your opinion. You might would like them to clarify the position they are taking or you would like to let them know the fact that you appreciate their point of view however, you have a slight difference between you.

Similar to:

There's no reason to believe you...

You're better informed than I am in this.

I can see the meaning you're trying communicate...

Your reasoning is logical for me...

It is possible that I am completely wrong in this instance...

I'm not able to find any an error...

A one of the subsequent "but" sentences (or something like it) will then be a follow-up to this sentence:

However, how do you think...

however I'd have thought the possibility...

But haven't you thought it...

But, in my personal knowledge...

However, I've come to the conclusion...

although it's also possible...

however, it's still possible...

However, this isn't however the situation...

but I'm still not certain.

For instance, let's use the following example:

There is no reason to doubt your accuracy But what happens is the possibility of rearranging the timetable? Do you think we may be successful?

It's not hard to see Sarah's rudeness towards you. But it could be that she was anxious over the performance.

I understand what you're saying However, I believe it was allowed to take dictionary to the exam.

It is possible that I am wrong however, I am convinced that Paris acts as the capital city of France.

You're far more educated about this subject than I am. However, as I've observed the stores usually close around 4.30 p.m. during the Sundays.

Chapter 4: Communicate Effectively

A good communication strategy can help maintain your healthy relationships avoid arguments as well as increase the chances getting what you want. Increase your ability to communicate through mastering the three elements consisting of listening actively, powerful speaking and body communication.

Practice attentive listening.

Listeners who are attentive seek out additional information and acknowledge that people's rights are not always respected, and allow others to disagree and offer assistance when necessary. Be sure to follow these tips and you'll soon be a superb listener

Shut up and take a seat. You shouldn't interrupt someone sharing a difficult or important story in telling them an interesting story about you, regardless of the relevance. Let them tell their story prior to looking for the reason they're feeling.

Don't judge others. Aid the person in overcoming their issues and give them solutions rather that judging them when you are asked for help.

Consider the possibility that they might have different views in comparison to your own. If someone seeks your advice or suggestions, don't think that they will follow all of your directions. While they might have turned to you seeking advice but they could find themselves disagreeing with the advice you've said. Let them decide on their own.

You can try open-ended questioning. Instead of asking questions that are yes or no ask open-ended questions that let the person you are talking to for them to lead the discussion in any direction they like. For instance, you could ask "Can I ask you about ...?" in order to obtain clarification.

Let the message be clear that you're paying to the situation. Make sure you understand the message through asking questions in the following steps as well as restating the facts in your own language. If they feel you're paying attention to them and they're more inclined to trust you and give you the benefit of doubt.

Be confident when you interact with other people.

There are generally three types of interaction:

Being angry and loud is one example of communication that is aggressive.

The inability to express one's personal thoughts, feelings, or desires is the hallmark of passive communications. It's not difficult to believe that the people around you are constantly stepping over you when they communicate in this manner.

The ability to express your thoughts, feelings and wishes without requesting to be satisfied is an example of assertive communication.

A strong personality lets you do things such as articulate your desires feelings, desires, and wants and seek the assistance of other individuals by making fair demands (while accepting their rights to refuse).

Protect your independence and individuality.

Refrain from social pressure and refuse to be influenced by social pressure and simply say "no" when asked for something.

Observe your nonverbal cues

Your tone and the volume the voice you use, along with your body language, facial expressions and emotional expressions, all impact how people perceive your message. The public is more likely to create barriers before even hearing the words you speak when you display an image of aggression such as when you fold the arms of your chest.

However, if you take a more approachable posture or speak in a relaxed manner, and appear relaxed and relaxed, your partner will be more relaxed and will feel more comfortable too.

If you're having trouble remembering the correct body language, perhaps this acronym could help you:

R - Be at peace Don't shake or sway around.

In order to adopt a stance that is open and to be open, you must say "O." (no arm crossed)

L Lean to the other person but not to far, but enough to display curiosity

Eye contact - Keep eye contact but do not stare

S - Contact to the person in question directly.

What should I do from this point?

Pay attention to how your body language can make others feel comfortable.

In order to develop your ability of communicating confidently, practice expressing your feelings, opinions and needs directly, without doubt.

Be able to start conversations with others by asking them about their lives and listening attentively and not interrupting as they talk.

For more positive and productive relationships, and less conflicts or miscommunications, you can try these ideas to improve communication

1. Take your words with thought.

An individual could get injured if they say an incorrect thing in the appropriate time. Take a look at a physician who provides an inaccurate medication to the patient as she lied about the prescription. An unintentional slip of the tongue during a trial in the tribunal could condemn an innocent person in prison for an extended period. When we interact with others, it is important be aware that your words could cause harm or even help. Therefore, take a moment to slow down, consider the response you will give, then be patient until the perfect time to speak.

You can learn more about the capacity of a person to be attentive by looking at their manner of speaking in their speech. When we're in a relationship with someone else, our thoughts and actions are at a similar level to the other's. When we're unconnected the conversations turn into words; we do not adjust our messages to the emotions of another person or mood. Instead, we rather relay the way we are experiencing. What's important is to pay attention. The conversation becomes monologue where one individual does all of the talking, while the other person is able to do nothing more then repeat what the other person has said.

Then, consider your thoughts before speaking and pay attentively to what other people are saying.

Make an efforts to be attentive and watch to someone else. The majority of people can hear something, but aren't paying focus on the details. The natural tendency is to contemplate how we should engage with a speaker instead of fully understanding what they're trying to communicate. You can become more attentive by reading this article.

3. Use your words to assist the person you are speaking to.

Speak to others to help those around you to help. Humans interact with each other for a myriad of motives. Sometimes, the goal of having a chat in a casual setting is to check out what happens as well as to observe how people are able to get along. As a person who listens there are times when you're lucky enough to be watching as a person is putting their thoughts out loud. Other times, data must be made available to serve a purpose. Other times it is the case that the speaker has expressed the need for assistance or feedback.

If you're engaging in idle conversation is always beneficial to offer some information to the person or to the discussion which adds value. Be sure to inquire for clarification in a respectful manner in case you're having difficulty understanding the conversation. If someone gives the opportunity to use something they're in need of or require, it could provide you with great help. The question "Are you telling me this to bounce ideas off of me or because you are asking for my help?" is an effective behavior to adopt in such situations. Consider the benefits the snuffing out of idle chatter can bring to your living.

Do not forget the possibility that your active listening could help another person as well as the conversation develop.

Fourth, always be sincere when you communicate.

The natural tendency of us is to lie and steal in our dealings with others. This is the behavior of those who master passive violence. In contrast we aspire to people who say it as they are. People who command respect are those who communicate honestly, regardless of whether they're male or female.

Truthfulness does not require employing hurtful language. The art of honesty can lead to many possibilities for your career and win the trust of others who are around you.

5. Recognize the ongoing awareness of the nonverbal language.

Although actions can be more powerful than words, they are much more clear in communicating their the meaning. Here are a few examples of non-verbal communication

Cues that are non-verbal as well as verbal

Face expressions are a way to communicate moods

Clothing and clothing

Behavior. Each action is a form of communication.

Know the significance of all three "V"s to effectively communicate:

The words spoken out loud are an example of spoken communication. However it is true that, like William Vermeulen stressed in his lecture, "most people focus just on the verbal portion thinking this is the message when it is merely part of the complete message,"

Vocals - including intonation resonance, volume.

The things that others see when they listen to you, like the facial expressions you use and your body expressions. Images convey information both consciously and in a non-conscious way to viewers. Based on the way you move your body, your thoughts can shine more brightly or disappear in the background.

Seventh, you must pick your words wisely and to deliver them at the right time.

Be clear about what you are saying and be sure to mean what you speak This is the old adage. Be aware that the words you speak could have a significant impact upon others. Continuously checking your words in order to ensure that they communicate your message is a good practice to adopt. The significance of your event dictates the exact words to be selected. In the case of launching an assault on the adversary, an officer soldier must communicate in a precise manner, but when you are playing tag with your daughter it is not as important to have accuracy in linguistics. Making a mistake at the wrong time can cause the same damage to an event or relationship in the same way as saying something wrong in the wrong context.

Making the right decision when it is the best time can be a significant influence on an individual's health. The impact could be far-reaching and positive effects.

Be assertive and diplomatic when in challenging situations.

It is important to learn to make use of words which are clear and tactful in addressing critique. Honesty does not have to mean tackiness.

Learn the most from inquiries. 9.

The majority of conversations are controlled by the one who is the one to ask the most questions. In reality, controlling everything does not always mean you're in control. In order to find the root of the issue and encourage people to talk about it ask the right questions. Utilize questions like "who," "what," "when," "where," "how," and "why" until your inquiries will be resolved.

Ten. Watch out for the opportunities to study about yourself, get answers or discover something regarding yourself.

For this, you must pause another person during crucial intervals and then directly inquire regarding their opinions.

11 Find an hour for a private registration.

The audience member seems to take a moment to think about the words stated. This is usually how the conversation will be if your words have touched an emotional chord.

However, don't make use of your silence as an excuse to send the other person mad. If you're feeling that the conversation getting too hard and you're not sure what to say, discuss the reasons you're not ready to say something and then stop the conversation.

Learn the goal of an upcoming meeting prior to the date.

If you're invited to meet someone, who you suspect that it's not an informal gathering it is best to politely demand to know what the intended goal of the meeting is beforehand.

Remember to note all pertinent details.

It is particularly important in situations where you are confronting an opponent confront-to-face, participating as a member of a high-risk committee or as a leader of a team. An ardent adherent of this rule, Winston Churchill took it very serious. This is a quote from one of his famous aphorisms: "I am a firm advocate of carrying out official business in the written word. ..." Note that I don't take responsibility for matters pertaining to national defense for which I'm believed to have made judgments until they have been documented in writing. I also require that any directives I issue must be written down or be verified promptly by writing.

14. Make sure everyone is informed on your goals and actions and share this info often.

15) Do not let anyone interfere with your activities.

People who interrupt may be doing so with motives However, they typically need to alter the topic or make their point clear. Because they aren't paying attention, people will disrupt. You must be attentive or else, efforts are futile. There are people who have a tendency to cut you off as they aren't thinking about them or other guests who are in the room. There is no way to not be disgusted when they do this. If they show little to any respect for each other, there's an extremely low chance of exchange. The two parties should be treated in a manner that is respectful. People will cut off you for lack of humility to recognize that what you are saying could be worth their time. In order to effectively communicate and work with their peers, they'll require a certain amount of humility.

If someone else keeps disrupting you, leave them to it.

Be sure to answer any those questions that require your attention.

Issues that are not resolved are common. They can resurface and create problems for relationships. If issues continue to arise when you've spoken about these issues, you should schedule an additional meeting. In general, it is best to concentrate on this issue in the next meeting.

Paraphrase in the 17th.

If the subject is significant, it might be helpful to write down what was discussed or ask your listener(s) perform the same. It could help determine whether both sides came to a mutually acceptable arrangement. By rephrasing the words of the person you disagree with stated and examining the other person to determine if you are on the same page can be a great method to ensure that you're at the same place.

Make sure to close the meetings by summarizing everything that was talked about.

Spend a few minutes following the meeting to review the discussions and determine whom is accountable for who is responsible for what.

If you're having difficulty communicating with someone, you can try to seek help from an outside source.

If you and a person are having difficulty communicating Try enlisting the help of a third party, or two. It is a tried and effective method of easing tensions that arise between parties that are always fighting. Be aware that it isn't an assurance of a peaceful conclusion in every case.

20. Be specific, but stay away from giving broad statements. Concrete instances should be accompanied by the abstract explanations. Professionals in effective communication advise using descriptive language as well as creating connections.

Get rid of any distractions that could distract your attention.

Remove anything that could interfere with the clarity of your conversation for the purpose of your talk. This can be done through a myriad of methods, like switching off your mobile and tablet, closing your laptop, and taking off the earpiece(s). Distractions can show another person that they're not crucial enough to merit your full concentration throughout the entire discussion and also stop your attention from being fully devoted to the discussion.

Distractions and distractions that could be brought up in conversation can be useful in various ways. There are many benefits to this:

Capable of carrying conversations in depth with people.

If you treat each other in a respectful manner, you'll increase the strength of your relationship.

Chances of success are greater.

It will be easier to concentrate more on your fellow participants and also the gathering's objectives.

It will be possible to recall the major elements of the conversation, as well as the conversation itself later point.

Chapter 5: Make Yourself an Influencer

The sweet, cinnamon-sugar scent is what comes to my mind immediately and recalls some of the people that had a significant influence on my life. Dad worked for KCBS Radio in San Francisco He baked a plethora of snickerdoodles every quarter. He brought them into the newsroom. My colleagues and I would push one another to get some.

Snickerdoodles aren't the most effective way to convince, however, radio icon Al Hart impressed me with his homemade treats, and instilled faith and trust within his staff.

The concept of influence has been unclear.

A leader's one of your main responsibilities is to influence other people. In the words of Oxford Dictionaries, influence is "the power to affect the personality, growth, or actions of another person or object, or the impact itself."

Being able to exert that influence in the lives of others shows that you are a leader. This is not an imposing force which entices people to follow your prefer, but rather faith in yourself that entices people to listen and inspires them to do something and encourages them to invest in to your ideas.

If you're hoping to move to the top of the corporate ladder What are the best ways to gain an influence? People who been the most influential in my life share many traits with me. In the end, I have some heroes with them.

In the event that I require inspiration for the next step, I often remember one of the three characters.

Long-time KCBS Radio Newscaster Al Hart demonstrated that good people always triumph. Hart made every effort to recall everyone's names as part of the team. He made it a point to hand-write greeting cards to celebrate birthdays as well as other celebrations.

Each day, he would set down and write a review the events of the day as well as be prepared to answer any difficult questions should they arise. He was honest and stated exactly what he thought. He was hopeful for only the best for his family members who were close to his heart. Many times I think about how my father encouraged me to be a hard worker as well as be kind to everyone else and have fun until I broke down. As I get older I'd like to become Al Hart; that has always been the guiding force behind my life.

Over the course of nearly 30 years, my aunt Marie ran for over thirty years the Chicago Office of 2 famous hand surgeons. All the while giving her nephews and nieces an endless amount of love, grace and courage. Every week during the last decade, I've been in touch with me to call. You can ask her about the story she saw in the newspaper or a new acquaintance she met at Trader Joe's or an unusual fruit she discovered at the market for farmers.

She inspired me to develop a love to cook at home, a love of arranging flowers in accordance with the size and colors, as well as the capacity to cultivate vegetables across the globe. She makes every effort to be a part of my life and is a part of the celebration of my accomplishments and sorrow of my loss. In a way she's my greatest friend.

Though I've never experienced the joy of meeting the author face-to-face her autobiographies along with her books and daily meditations give me the impression that I have met her very well. Even though she was rejected for nearly 10 years, she continued working on her writing. Therefore, you should raise your hand even if you've not had the pleasure of reading or watching "A Wrinkle in Time."

The compassion she shows for people and her capacity to bridge the two as well as her love with her family and friends and her peace when standing on a rock next to streams and her confidence sharing her thoughts all inspired me to follow her steps. Each time I open one of her books and go through it, I find myself longing to have the same qualities as her.

When you think about your heros You may discover that they have traits that you would like to have. Think about your role models to determine the road to becoming a leader. Find out the best route for you.

Top 4 Qualities of an Effective Influencer

"Influencers" are a word that is now in the consciousness of people due to the social media. Achieving influence in the workplace does not have much in common with the type of influence. After experiencing the immense effect of influential people on your daily life, it is now possible to recognize the value of real inter-personal connection.

These are the four qualities that make an effective person stand out:

They are willing to take the risk. People who are deliberate stand out as they're always ready move on to the next level whether in their work or in everyday life. They keep a long-term view to think about when planning their days and establish the daily goals. They are also careful with their words, understanding how powerful words can be in persuasiveness.

They conduct their research prior to making speeches and collaborate to give an exceptional service. Additionally, they keep the same level of excellence through regular participation with the above mentioned behaviors.

In the end that they're connected. You'll be able to feel welcomed and respected when you're in the presence of someone who is powerful. There are times when you may be asked questions or receive feedback to make to feel more at home in the group of trust.

The link above should serve as an opportunity to remind yourself that although they're at the helm but they're not going to do it on their own. This is why cooperating with them is the best option, and it is possible to feel positive about the outcome.

They're strong like nails. Someone with influence knows that there are times when plans fail to work out. If they are faced with chaos they're willing to put on their apron to come up with an idea. They're also interested in discussion about the strategy together with the other members of the group.

It is evident that they're looking forward to the long-term by the fact that they're willing try something new and are honest about the difficulties they're facing. If faced with challenges an influential person could take advantage of it as a chance to rethink their strategies and method of action.

Learning is a continuous process that continues all through their lives. If you're in the company of someone who is influential You can sense how far ahead of them are due to their dedication to their personal growth. They don't make a big deal about their forthcoming arrival as they're aware of more to come across the horizon.

A desire to learn will drive you to take a class and stay up all night to master a new piece of software, or explore an interesting business-related book. Learning solely for the sake of learning adds to their level of enjoyment.

Complete guide for maximizing your impact at work (or elsewhere)

Now is the time to take your first step. If you're looking to be more powerful, these eight steps will change your relationships with all those you meet.

Do not interrupt me when I'm speaking. One of the most important aspects to listening is having a calm and peaceful mental state. The act of listening requires complete attention. Concentrate on what's being spoken rather than on the things you'd like to respond with. It's good to establish a habit of having a paraphrased version of what someone else says. The fact that you took the time to repeat this again will show your friend that you are listening to what they said.

Alternatively, "I understood what you were saying ...."" -- in order to make sure you've understood the subject matter and show that you're committed to this process. In this way, if you're unsure about the subject, you'll know instantly and will be able to seek clarification. Being able to make someone take note of the things you say is an incredibly rare thing that is likely to boost your credibility with that person.

You must be honest. It is a matter of being in line with your character and your actions are logical because they're grounded within a sense that is based on personal respect for your integrity. Integrity is a word that means "completeness. "integrity" comes from the Latin word "integer," which means "complete." Being honest means being you everywhere, whether in the workplace, at home, or even in the grocery checkout line.

The actions you take affect those who are around you and you're aware.

Furthermore, you're the only person that can be identified at any time. Integrity also implies that your beliefs, behavior as well as your words, are in harmony with each other, regardless of what the situation.

Keep your promises. If you want others can count on you, it is essential be true to your word. Make sure to send the response to the person by tomorrow, at 9 a.m. and as you promised. If you're not able to react immediately, tell them know that you're studying the situation and when you'll be in a position to respond. If people trust you, it increases your credibility.

Let others be let others be heard. Avoid rushing into by introducing yourself or making a idea, however tempting it could be. If you take time to be attentive and take note of the opinions of your colleagues they will gain the ability to express the thoughts they have in mind. When you allow people to share their thoughts to the conversation, they feel important and appreciated.

It is important to take health care of your health. Monitoring yourself regularly helps you to stay focused at the present moment and serve as a model for those in your life. A state of wellness is one which is in complete emotional, mental physical, and spiritual well-being. Do you exercise regularly and consume healthy food? Have you ever tried to manage your thoughts? Who do you turn to for a problem you need to talk about? How often are you practicing meditation and mindfulness? Your ability to discern the needs of people around you is dependent on the awareness you have of their requirements.

You must ensure that your talents remain relevant. Stay informed of the most current developments in your field, if are looking to influence. If you need to, you are able to swiftly alter your course if you need to make a change. This is evident that you appreciate and accept changes as the norm in your life.

A "how things are done" or "I know best" mentality isn't a viable one at work today. If you stay on the lookout at trends and forecasts You can modify and improve your current expertise and abilities. You're aware of the strategies to boost your company's effectiveness and position on the marketplace.

Concentrate your attention on at the place it is needed. By separating yourself from petty issues or rivals can distinguish you as an influential person. This is because you are significantly more about improving the effectiveness and efficiency of other people than regarding your own personal growth and advancement. Your team is achieving more success through the development of strategies, and performing it in a manner which sets new standards for the highest level of excellence.

Contact other people. In order to entice people's attention in your career You must be able to communicate with them on a personal and intimate degree. Each person you work with is a person you know, and you're aware of their flaws and the best way to show the best of them. You face challenges but celebrate triumphs with an entire team. Your teammates see through you, and they believe that they know you well.

A final tip: demonstrate passion. Showing genuine enthusiasm about the work you do is a tried and true way of drawing like-minded people in your cause, and persuading them to join to your cause. Exuberance and passion are infectious when they're genuine, and it is evident.

For you to gain many fans, you require more than a history of success and an unwavering faith. At work the effects could be profound and influence your choices, the direction of the organization, and the company's culture and building the trust and respect of your employees.

When you are expanding the sphere of influence you have You may not be aware that your actions can affect the people around you. You could, for instance, be an extremely hard-working individual that is adamant about your work and is always willing to give 100 percent regardless of how long the process is or how challenging the work at hand could be. While no one's looking, you can gain knowledge and develop. As you reflect, it becomes evident that you're dissecting the idea of the impact.

Snicker doodles By the way they are an excellent idea at any time.

Chapter 6: How Do You Convince People To Be Real Quickly?

George C. Parker has been hailed as the most persuasive American ever by a few. Parker has, for a long time was able to convince the public at least twice per week to believe that he was the Brooklyn Bridge's owner. When they placed their faith on him, he'd offer to sell them the bridge. Most often, those who fell for his fraud would discover the truth only after they were imprisoned for knowingly putting toll barriers along "their" bridge.

Parker isn't the best instance of integrity He certainly knew how to convince individuals to view things in a certain way. As a professional, business owner or professional once you've achieved the art of persuasive.

What was the most recent instance you were a victim of verbal bullying to accept an argument? It's never happened, or at the minimum, extremely likely. Even though you appear as if you're giving up but in reality, you're remaining true to your beliefs. It's hard to not be annoyed with the individual and hold anger towards them.

However, the opposite strategy will be more effective: Listen well and pay the person the full attention of your time. You should allow them to go at first. Once you've decided in that you want to convince them You could say something along the lines of "Please share your opinions with me about X. What are they, and could you send them to me?"

The following is a the list of possible replacements for:

"As such, I anticipate that you will provide some insightful commentary about Y. How receptive you are to talking about them remains to be seen."

"You have some strong opinions on this matter. I'm interested in your justifications."

Inquiring, "Could you kindly explain your thinking procedure?"

"Come on, I want to hear about Z. Please share your thoughts with me."

2.) In accord with their reasoning

The saying "fight fire with fire" can be a successful method of being influential. As per research studies the most effective way to influence people is to follow the same way of thinking that the person whom you're trying to influence as opposed to trying to persuade the person to your method of thinking.

If your opponent is thinking rationally, you ought to use the same method. If they're relying on their own feelings emotional arguments can likely convince them.

Think about a potential customer who's in the middle of changing vendors. They've used the same vendor for about 10 years, and they've been able to have nothing but good experience.

Avoid starting with an argument based on logic like, "Switching to our product would decrease your production time by 10%," because they'll likely deny this because it contradicts their emotions. The argument isn't likely to resonate with anyone.

It could be something along the lines of "I am aware of that. We strive to get the same amount of trust and support from all of our customers. We'll assign an additional account manager for free during your initial year. They will ensure that everything runs smoothly and that you're comfortable.

Are you having trouble distinguishing between various types of arguments? Pay attention to the words employed by the other party.

The words used to explain logic

Analyze

Calculate\Conclude

Compel\Determine

Discover

Find\Gauge

Hypothesize

Predict

Reveal\Think\sValidate

Verify

The words used to explain emotions

Believe\Feel\Guess

Imagine

suppose\suspect

The third is to applaud their style of thinking.

When a potential customer makes an argument that you are in agreement with, say "It seems like you've put some thought into this."

The study found that those who felt they'd paid consideration to a dual-sided message proved more certain of their conclusions as compared to those convinced that they had considered the issue less. This means that potential customers tend to stick with an idea if they're convinced that they've spent an extended period of time constructing the conclusion.

How much could it be effective? Consider a scenario where an interested client states something along the lines of "The adaptability of your software is particularly enticing as we anticipate growth of 150% in the following year."

This can be used to your advantage by using something along the lines of "It sounds like you've thought about what you'll need as you scale."

They'll be more convinced that the product you offer is an ideal match when they've had their beliefs established.

Do you want to investigate the possibilities? Try:

"You raise some valid arguments."

"I have a lot to think about because of what you said."

The method you used to arrive at the conclusion that you reached blew me away.

I admire your ability to look at things from multiple angles.

4.) Argument against it

Don't wait to allow the opposing party to make a counter argument; you must actively push your opponent to make a statement.

The argument may not make sense in the least. An analysis of the meta-analysis of research with 20,111 individuals but it's clear that arguments with two sides have more credibility than ones that are one-sided.

If you make a counter argument that you do not then challenge your argument, the strategy you are pursuing is likely to fail.

Inform the customer that "Our software for accounting does not allow customers to connect with accounts. This is a feature I'm certain you'll enjoy.

By putting everything out in the open will increase the credibility of your business immediately. However, you shouldn't not answer any questions So, you should continue with things like "We choose to provide automatic, recurring paying instead so that after you've set it up, you'll never have to worry about payments again." In addition, users don't need to sign on for new services in order for checking their accounts and can do it directly from their email mailboxes.

This solution will carry greater weight because you've gained the trust of your prospect instead of having to wait for them to raise the issue.

Perhaps you'll raise a topic that you doubt they would have considered raising by themselves. It may be odd, but if you successfully discredit the opposition this will boost your credibility, and help your argument more convincing.

For instance as an example, you might say "A security concern may be on your mind.

Initially, a great deal of your clientele will fall into this category. Do you have it in mind right now?"

If they do respond affirmatively (and almost always be, in order to avoid appearing uninformed or reckless) You could then say something along the lines of "An extremely worrying situation, in fact. Actually, according to Consumer Protection Agency, our gadget increases the security of your home because …"

You could make a better case for yourself if spend the time to construct your arguments before tackling the opposition.

The Fifth Commandment: Always Speak Clearly and Explicitly

An extremely difficult study on the Munchhausen Trilemma was once imposed on me by my philosopher-brother and he promised me that it would change my view of life for the better.

After about a month after which he asked my thoughts. For example, I told him: "I couldn't comprehend more than 10 words in a succession."

This is the lesson to learn that no matter how convincing your argument is, if person can comprehend the concept.

It's the same when you're presenting a complex psychology theory or the advantages of your latest offering. Jargon, five-dollar words or industry buzzwords may appear impressive, however they can only make your customers confused and lead loss of sales.

In this regard, it is important to make your message as concise as you can in your communications. Example:

What's wrong: We've created an instantaneous pipeline that absorbs the entire stream of tweets, process the tweets, and provides an efficient real-time decision making platform built on sentiment and multi-dimensional analysis on tweets related to a particular campaign.

Right: Our app collects data of Twitter profiles, process it and then displays results on a simple screen. Always have up-to-date data available for making the right choices.

Which one is more convincing? The second argument is more convincing.

If you're not certain that you're using the right language try putting yourself into the perspective of a fifth-grade student. This way will ensure that the words and explanations that you select are easy to understand.

Once you're familiar with these tried and true techniques of convincing, winning over your clients will be a less daunting fight. Utilize your talents to your advantage and do not harm anyone Also do not try to sell bridges.

Have you ever you had a person who held absolute control over you? Yes, I've always dreamed of this rare power.

A myriad of books and workshops will reveal how to effectively persuade. While these articles and books assist in understanding how to persuade however, they usually ignore simple methods to get your message across to other people.

Persuasion doesn't require you to be born a salesperson. In order to increase the chances to succeed, you'll need not do anything more difficult other than paying focus on the basics.

First, you must make sure that the words you use have the potential to create an impact.Words that trigger a response are crucial in the pitch. Certain phrases could be employed to build compelling and concise arguments.

The term "car accident" might conjure pictures of various kinds of crashes involving motor vehicles. But, you shouldn't consider the fact that there are a lot of crashes every day as an argument for car insurance. There's a good chance that you'll say that thousands die every single day because from car accidents.

The word "death" evokes more emotion than "accident," and marketers employ this advantage constantly.

Some of the most persuasive English phrases are listed below.

Don't wear business attire. Avoid making use of condescending words.

Although no one will be there to greet you dress well, it can help you feel comfortable. A negative consequence of looking the most stylish on the block could be that you end being a victim of gossip or shaming people that are actually superior to your level.

It's easy to fall into this trap since we are prone to praising another person whenever we believe that we are in an advantage when we are in a conversation. This isn't difficult even. However, it's likely that you'll lose your clients if the process isn't simple or you're not effectively communicating.

Be aware that who you're pitching your idea to is a higher level on the corporate ladder than you. They are able to decide to say "no" if they so prefer. To maintain the advantage when discussing the issue it is important not to let anyone else to be aware that you're talking to them in a negative way. can be an obstacle to a contest neither one either of you would want to participate in. Be careful not to cross the line of the two.

Third, consider the future.

The confidence can be established quickly through the use of the present in the present. Being confident that you're moving forward and you are ready to follow through on the promises you made reassures others.

Making use of the term "will" is a simple technique to achieve this. Utilizing phrases such as "We will" and "Then we'll do this" will aid the person in accepting the notion that it is likely to happen.

But, be careful not to over-aggressive. In as much as you are able avoid making decisions on behalf of the person who is making them and instead, engage in a candid dialog about options that are available and the possible results.

Don't be visible.

What's out to reach are things which people would like the most. Make sure to remind them that this chance won't be around forever and that the opportunity would be lost in the event that they did not take the opportunity now.

In the case of promoting products it is extremely efficient. Making the new item appear as if it is going to sell rapidly is a typical technique for marketing. It appeals to those with a "Get it now while you can!" mentality.

5. Find the most suitable way to present your idea.

The person you're asking to perform things they're probably not interested in performing (yet). Therefore need to set up the right environment for your talk.

Discover the personality of the individual through observation.

If you can offer the option of asking them if they would prefer email over phone calls could be a good idea.

Sometimes I'll meet one who is more comfortable with texting than real-time conversations. Keep this in mind when you pick a platform that concentrates on the intended audience, and not on your.

Make use of a language that they can understand.

It's not the best idea to swoop in and complete an individual's words. It's because your power on their thoughts is decreased by the way you use your mind in order to "speak" for them.

Anyone who enjoys the sensation of being intruded upon?

Take note of the tone of voice and behavior. You have to determine which strategy you apply. Is the vocabulary sometimes lost? Similar to that the language should be used. Are they using prepositions to create sentence ends and jokes? It is recommended to adopt a similar casual method.

It is important to be able to connect not just the language used, but the voice tone and facial expression. If you notice that they are more active in their way of communicating like gesturing or speaking with their hands then it may be a good idea to follow the same method. If they appear hesitant and shut off (arms crossed, etc.) you should not make any explicit gestures of the affection.

It also is effective when you are speaking to large crowds. Check to see if you are able to see the room, and work out what they like about your presentations. Learn what's worked and then apply the information.

7 Avoid unneeded pauses when speaking.

Each time you say "um" or "uh," you are discrediting the person who is listening to your message. If what you're trying to say is vital but it will not make any distinction.

Continue to flow with ideas and words. One of the easiest ways to accomplish this is to give an idea of what you'll say prior to when you speak and then practicing your own speech in the comfort of your the home.

Eight, aid them by helping them out in some way.

As a child when you were young, you likely have told your parents the way you felt about the way they treated you before you even asked them to do some thing. It is a fact that we learn in the beginning that people are more likely to aid us when they are helping us in exchange in exchange for something we've given them.

This is even before you present your plan. Making a connection on social media with favorable intentions will improve the chance of the other party to aid you later on.

Because you cannot be certain of the person monitoring you, it's fair to repay the favor. I've done a unasked for favor by sharing the link to an amazing website in this forum. Due to the rise in sales, the person who received it was so pleased of me that they even gave me some gratis stuff. While I hadn't expected to receive it, and they weren't feeling that they were obliged to do so but they did and this strengthened our bonds and opened the way for the possibility of future collaboration.

9. Find out how to manage time.

It is akin to the first point regarding being aware of your target audience. Find out about them and how you are able to best reach them.

For instance, some executives might be totally exhausted on Friday, because they had been overwhelmed in the beginning in the work week. If you are trying to convince someone that Thursday is the best time to make it happen.

Because you have a better understanding of them Friends and family members can be more convincing. Chances of success rise if you pick the best time to speak with them.

Do not be afraid to share your thoughts and emotions.

The goal is to win the trust of another person. The questions are all asked But how did you achieve this?

Discuss the change of your belief system from the point you used to be and what you're currently. Encourage them with an inspiring story about your journey to education. If you can time the conversation or pitching in this manner and reassure anyone else you have thought it through and can meet their needs.

11. Rephrase what they've spoken about.

Be sure to show that you value what your opponent is telling you by responding to their remarks and appreciating their feelings. One way to check your thoughts is to say something like "If I'm interpreting you right, then you're stating that you consider this to be significant because of X, Z, and Y. Yes, I understand it and my thinking is AB or C.

I guarantee you that you'll discover this helpful even if you're not in the business of letters.

12 - Develop to the climax of sensation.

emotional responses such as enthusiasm and awe are better left to evolve naturally throughout the course of conversation. Avoid trying to infect them with the excitement they do not experience.

It is best to save the bulk of your energy-driven language until the final part to your presentation. This helps it appear authentic and build on strong arguments in the light of the discussion that preceded it.

Chapter 7: Listen To the Views of Other People

Recognizing the value of the views of other people is essential to being respectful.

Respect for each person is something that we must develop as we age. Being respectful of other viewpoints is a difficult art. You must have faith in your abilities, as well as be able to control your emotions and tolerance, compassion in the face of injustice, fairness, and kindness. This is also the case for overtly stated and hidden convictions.

Different types of disdain can be displayed to individuals according to one's perception of the person. The first is dismissing the thoughts and opinions of others without a second thought. It is also possible to believe that they are in agreement with our opinions.

The right to respect the viewpoints of other is not a requirement for compromising the views we hold. What we must be able to agree is that everybody is entitled to your own perspective and opinion of the world.

Everyone deserves to be heard whenever they share their opinions.

The beliefs we hold are an essential aspect of our identity.

This is why people often view the criticism we receive from others as a rejection. In this case it's not difficult to become defensive and angry, which can stop further conversations. That's why we must be able to adhere to a set of agreements and, when practical and appropriate take these actions:

The first step is to consider the essence of another's perspective, even if it is necessary to justify your belief in the viewpoint. It's true that what you're saying might be correct generally, however there are instances where...

Be aware that what you're getting is reasonable even if you don't agree with the idea. "However," he said, "although that concept has merits ,..."

Consider that your view of the world could alter based upon new data. You might say "I do not know. It doesn't make sense However, maybe there's something more happening here than I am able to see at the moment.

Fourth, use the lens metaphor frequently. It is possible to say, "Yes, but if you take a moment and think about the issue from a different angle ..."

This is a list of qualified disagreement. This can be more beneficial as opposed to a full-blown disagreement. The severity of your problem by employing these types of disagreements. However, if contrary to what you've read you find the controversial opinion offensive, feel in the position of rejecting the argument outright. This isn't right and I'm sorry to do that. On the other hand, "I find this viewpoint offensive. This is in direct contradiction to my morals, as you can imagine.

If we are in disagreement with one another, our reactions vary depending upon the situation, context, and the activity.

If, for example, you don't agree with the idea that more funds is needed to be given to private schools instead of within the government sector, then you might come across the debate. It is possible to present a rational argument in an PTA or town-hall meeting. If you're an invited guest at the dinner at the table, it's polite to not discuss this issue, and instead go on. Also it is important to weigh the significance of expressing your views against your hosts efforts to create a friendly environment of friendship. Most of the time, a meal isn't the ideal opportunity or time to debate issues of politics.

A lot of people appear like they are the only ones who agree with them, even though they aren't. Such a type of preconceived notions of sharing can result from feelings of insensitivity or may be an a deliberate (though subdued) effort to say, "If you don't think like me, you should start now." However, it's still bullying regardless of the reason.

Somewhere or other there has been a time when we've all suffered the consequences of someone else's assumption of their viewpoint. Each time I'm attracted to the exhausting task of trashing different forms of digital media. There is always people who feel the need to convince me that TV can be harmful for me and all of us. The argument is that it's an indisputable fact that demands little investigation as it's considered valid by all people who has a functioning brain. That means that I'm expected to accept the critique. But the point is that it frustrates me to be swept into a club I've have never been interested in joining.

People who make that "I'm sure you're one of us" assumption, they are assumption for us and are unwilling to think about the possibility that they could be mistaken. In the absence of a better word it's rude.

People who don't agree with you might choose to keep their distance in order to maintain peace. They might feel too afraid to come up against you it is possible that they would refrain from speaking. It is possible that they will be angry in the end when they realize they're making the assumption that they have a common view, when it is not the case. Be gentle with them.

Make it clear that your opinions are just thoughts, do not represent gospel truths. Let people discuss their issues and to express their opinions.

The query "What do you think?" is one of the easiest or least obtrusive, but the most shrewd phrases that have ever been heard. We should be flexible in how we employ this phrase.

When we are attentive to someone else's view, it's possible to discover something new.

It is possible that we will realize our judgement was not so sound as we thought.

It seems to me that when they are confronted by someone with views different from your own, the overwhelming majority of people would like to "win" the debate (of of course, that could be my impression as a result of what I've observed in social media websites like Reddit or Twitter in which it appears like users are becoming more hostile towards one another whenever they come across views and opinions that are different from their personal views).

However, I'm not convinced that this is the most effective method to handle people who don't agree with your views and you can stay away from being rude and confrontational by choosing to engage in a discussion rather. The world isn't always clear as there's every day more than one approach to comprehend your surroundings So why not make the most of it to expand your perspective?

It is better to try to understand the other's view and point of view in the matter rather than attempt to dominate their perspective with your own, and subsequently ignore the other person's perspective.

It isn't possible to grow in your life by fighting with others and you grow as a person through being open to different perspectives. How can you make the most from the reality that each person experiences a unique set of experiences that cause people to view things differently? Make an effort to have a conversation with others whose beliefs that you don't agree with and even simply asking "That's fascinating, why do you feel that way?" To hear their thoughts and think about their viewpoint.

If you are able to understand the perspective of someone else and accept their rationales to support their position isn't a requirement to take them on or you've been defeated This simply means that you're open to listening other views. It implies that you are open to listening to opposing sides of the debate because you are aware the possibility of benefits to engaging in this manner.

Do not feel pressured to respond so strongly whenever you encounter people with an opinion or perspective differs from your own; Most people don't have a problem with you to argue or annoy them (of obviously, occasionally it could be and that's fine, but it's generally not the reason why people disagree or have different views).

Do's

Ask questions further, using phrases such as "That's intriguing," etc. What's it about that experience?

Try to engage in conversations that are respectful and respectful. Always make sure you are prepared to justify your decision as well as why you believe that you are right. However, be prepared be prepared to hear your opponent out.

In your interactions with other people It is important to build the conversation on facts, instead of feelings or personal thoughts.

Make sure you are able to maintain your posture with a calm and steady manner.

Be aware that you and the other party do not have a disagreement on only one point; you're not trying to get into an argument against the other person.

Find a middle way. There's probably some aspects of the matter on which you and your opponent are able to agree, regardless of your discord. Knowing these aspects can aid you in your efforts to communicate with your counterpart as well as be able to gently express your frustrations regarding other matters.

Instead of saying "You," try adding "I," as in, "I understand ..." Do not make your partner think that they're being slandered Make sure to show you're open to hearing the other person's perspective, regardless of whether you don't agree.

Be attentive to the person you are talking to. Individuals who read only the headline, but ignore what's in the body cause me to feel uncomfortable. You shouldn't be merely listening to soundbites or summary of what another person is saying. Instead concentrate on the actual meaning behind what they're speaking about.

It is acceptable to agree on a compromise at certain points. Collaboration and friendship don't necessarily need unanimous agreement regarding every subject.

Do not be afraid to quit an interaction if you notice the tension increasing or someone else becomes unfriendly. A threatening attitude won't convince someone else to alter their minds; instead, it could cause a more intense tension when they react to the insult by using your personal.

Don'ts

Do not dismiss someone else's point of view simply because it doesn't align with your view. It could be you that is 'wrong', or, even more specifically the truth is somewhere in between your viewpoint and that of the other individual's perspective.

Do not resort to physical violence as it will only create tensions.

Inflexibility makes it difficult to learn from other people and prevents your from getting the most out of each encounter. Every person, including those who that you don't agree with is able to impart knowledge So it's essential to be open to the viewpoint of others even if you are planning to turn it over in the future.

You don't have to worry about getting as the winner in this debate. Be open to the possibility that you're likely to find some valuable lesson to be learned from your opponent If you feel that the conversation isn't working be polite and end the discussion prior to the discussion turning nasty.

Do not be scared of conflict or conflict; honest disagreement can be more beneficial than an untruthful agreement.

Do not only search to find and witness evidence that reinforces the preconceived ideas. One of the best ways to grow as a human being is to to look at the arguments and ideas you previously dismissed. Simply because you are able to consider the opposite view does not necessarily mean that you must take it on board.

It's ineffective to invest trying to persuade people to agree with your opinions and be in agreement with your views. If you're trying to make people talk with one another and you're done.

There are numerous ways that can use conflict for your benefit, and disagreements can provide an excellent opportunity to work with others and develop as an individual. Look for areas where you can agree in order to build a solid foundation of trust. You can then improve your communication skills when you have differences. If you and a couple begin to argue however, that doesn't mean that you must stay the in that way.

Chapter 8: The Psychology of Likeability

Do you have any questions about how some people are generally liked while other people struggle to be connected to others?

The truth is that there's actually quite a bit of psychological reasons why people are drawn to the other.

The first and most important thing is that the majority of people like those that are like them.

This is known as the "similarity-attraction" principle.

When we get to know those who have the same interests in values, beliefs, or experience We feel a sense of belonging and comfort.

This is the reason it is crucial when it comes to building relationships.

Another aspect that determines the way we view others is the physical appearance.

Research has shown that individuals tend to fall in love with people who look attractive physically.

Physical attractiveness can be linked to positive characteristics like kindness, intelligence and trustworthiness.

It is important to keep in mind that the definition of attractiveness is an individual thing and can differ in accordance with personal and cultural desires.

What someone might find attractive might differ for other people.

In addition, they tend to be drawn towards people who inspire them to feel better of themselves.

It is also known as "auto-verification" or the "self-verification" principle.

When we are able to validate our thoughts or opinions and opinions, we feel happier with those around us.

That's why listening to your partner and showing empathy are essential when it comes to establishing relations.

Contrarily the other hand, many people disapprove of those who undermine the self-confidence of their own or challenge their convictions.

It is also known by"social comparison" or the "social comparison" principle. If we feel less than or doubts our assumptions, we could be affronted or defensiveness in their direction.

Another crucial factor that affects the perception of likability is how socially privileged.

People are drawn to people with good social standing or who have a reputation for being successful.

The reason for this is that social standing can be linked to positive characteristics like intelligence, competence as well as influence.

It's also important to keep in mind that it's not solely about being like attractive, appealing, and effective.

Strong relationships require the ability to communicate well with empathy as well as being able to manage the complexities of conflict and tough circumstances.

The psychology that underlies what makes people feel a certain way is complex and multi-faceted.

It is a mix of variables like physical attractiveness, similarity and validation. It also involves public status and capabilities.

When we understand these aspects and focusing on making ourselves more appealing and build better relationships with people we meet in our daily lives.

The Importance of Body Language and Nonverbal Communication

Did you know about the expression, "actions speak louder than words"?

The fact is that this is applicable to communications.

The body language of our friends and the non-verbal signals are crucial to the way we interact with people and is essential to build good connections.

In the first place, body language is able to communicate a lot of information regarding how we feel as well as what thoughts we're having.

For instance, arms that are crossed could signal defensiveness or irritation A smile, for instance, can signal happiness and warmth.

When we are attentive to these signs by paying attention, we will be able to better comprehend the motives and feelings of people around us.

Second, the way we talk to others can be a factor in our perception by others.

Studies have shown that people who communicate with confidence and open body language are generally viewed as trustworthy, more appealing and knowledgeable.

The reason is that our body language can communicate the level of our trust, enthusiasm as well as engagement.

Communication via non-verbal means also play significant roles in how we establish and keep relationships.

By making eye contact is a sign you're engaged and genuinely interested in what another person is saying.

Making appropriate gestures and facial expressions, we can express our feelings and establish trust.

Furthermore, nonverbal cues may assist in controlling and regulating social interactions.

Like, nodding and smiling may indicate agreement and acceptance, whereas a tense eye may indicate displeasure or displeasure.

Through the use of appropriate nonverbal cues by using appropriate nonverbal cues, we can make a happy and more comfortable environment for social interaction.

But, it's crucial to remember that non-verbal and body language communications can be complicated and can be misinterpreted easily.

In other words, someone who feels anxious or uneasy might display the body language which is believed to be as a sign of defensiveness or lack of interest.

It is important to take into account the context as well as multiple clues when interpreting body language as well as non-verbal messages.

The importance of body language as well as non-verbal communications cannot be understated.

They are crucial for efficient communications and for building relationships.

Paying close attention to our physical language as well as non-verbal cues as well as being mindful of the body language and nonverbal cues of others to improve our communication skills, and thus become more successful in establishing and keeping relations.

The Power of Positivity And Attitude

Did you know about the expression, "attitude is everything"?

When it comes to attracting people positive mindset is essential.

The way we conduct ourselves can significantly influence the way we're perceived by others and has a major effect on the quality our relations.

In the first place, having an attitude of positivity can assist draw others in our direction.

People naturally gravitate towards people who exude positivity and joy.

If we're optimistic and upbeat it's easy to draw people with these characteristics.

Furthermore, having a positive mindset helps make a positive and sociable environment.

If we approach social occasions positive and enthusiastically We'll be more likely to foster a warm and enjoyable environment.

This will help ensure that others are comfortable and involved, which can lead to better relationships.

An optimistic attitude can aid in building resilience and be able to handle challenging scenarios.

If we tackle the challenges with a positive attitude it is easier to come up with solutions and overcome challenges.

This will help build our confidence, and also help others take the same steps.

It's also important to remember that having positive attitudes don't just mean that you ignore or deny the negative feelings or circumstances.

It's crucial to be aware of the negative feelings however, it is important to process them with a positive and constructive manner.

This could involve reframe difficult situations in a positive way, seeking help from friends and family, as well as practicing self-care.

Apart from being positive It's equally crucial to have a growing mentality.

This means embracing difficulties and failures as an opportunity to learn and grow.

When we embrace a growth mindset and embracing growth, we will inspire others to be the same and foster a culture that encourages continual learning and improvement.

The power of positive attitude and positivity is not to be underestimated.

If we approach social events with enthusiasm and positivity We can draw others in and help create a happier and sociable environment.

If we keep a positive outlook and a positive outlook, we are able to build our confidence and motivate others to follow suit.

When we prioritize positivity and an attitudes, we are able to be magnets for people and create powerful, long-lasting connections.

Chapter 9: Developing Charisma

Charisma is an attribute which some individuals appear to naturally possess however, it's also something that can be developed or developed.

Charisma is the result of a mix of traits and behavior that draw people towards us. This could be a great benefit in our personal as well as professional life.

Here are some suggestions to help you develop and enhance your personality:

Practice active listening:

The most charismatic people tend to be excellent listeners.

They listen to their fellows they ask questions and are interested in the opinions of others.

Learn to listen actively through focusing on what the individual is talking, asking questions that are open to interpretation in a summary of the conversation to prove that you comprehend.

Be authentic:

Charisma is all about being authentic and real.

The public can tell if they are not being sincere or fake. It's essential to remain authentic and don't try to put in a show.

Take pride in your own unique talents and don't be scared to be yourself.

Develop confidence:

People who are confident radiate confidence which attracts others.

For building confidence, concentrate on your accomplishments and strengths as well as self-care. challenge yourself by getting outside of your comfortable zone.

Use body language effectively:

Body language is an integral aspect of charisma.

Make sure to use a confident and open body language. This includes keeping eyes in contact with each other, sitting straight and using the appropriate gestures.

Take note of body language of other people and adapt your body language to match theirs.

Do some storytelling practice:

People who are charismatic tend to be great storytelling experts. Make sure you tell stories that are entertaining funny, relatable, and humorous.

Utilize storytelling to make connections with other people and develop connections.

Build emotional intelligence:

The concept of emotional intelligence is to be conscious of the emotions we experience as well as the feelings of others.

People who are charismatic have a high emotional intelligence and have the ability to be in touch with people emotionally.

Develop empathy, emotional control and social abilities to increase your emotional mental.

Make sure you are positive

People who are charismatic have an optimistic attitude and perspective about the world.

Look for the positive of people and situations, and maintain an optimistic attitude, even in difficult circumstances.

If you follow these guidelines by following these tips, you can build and enhance your personality.

Always remember, it's about expressing yourself, gaining confidence and interacting with people on a real scale.

Through practice and perseverance With practice and persistence, you'll become attracted to people and create solid, lasting friendships.

The Importance of Authenticity And Self-confidence

Confidence and honesty are among the most essential traits in the process of developing strong relationships and being popular with people.

We'll take a look at what makes these attributes essential.

Authenticity:

Being authentic means being honest to yourself, and not attempting to be somebody you're not.

If we're genuine and authentic, we can be able to connect with people at a deeper level since we're expressing our authentic selves.

The authenticity of a person can aid in building confidence and trust. These are crucial to establishing lasting relations.

The public can tell the signs that someone is not sincere or fake. It could be an indication of a negative impression.

However If someone is genuine and authentic, it could be refreshing and appealing.

When we embrace our authentic selves and expressing ourselves authentically by being authentic, we are able to attract those who respect and admire ourselves for the person we truly are.

Self-confidence:

The ability to be confident is another crucial factor in order to become an attraction to people.

If we're confident about the abilities of ourselves and others and we radiate a sense of enthusiasm and charm that's appealing to those around us.

People are drawn by people who feel confident and self-assured. confident.

Self-confidence is also a great way to assist us in conquering difficulties and be willing to take chances.

When we trust in ourselves and believe in ourselves, we're more inclined to accept new problems and break beyond our comfort zones.

This could lead to the development of our personal and professional lives, that in turn can attract other people that are influenced by our drive and confidence.

It's also important to keep in mind that self-confidence does not refer to being arrogant, or a disdainful of other people.

True self-confidence is a equilibrium between self-assurance and humbleness.

It's about having confidence in your strengths, while accepting the possibility of learning and development.

The bottom line is that authenticity and confidence in yourself are the most important qualities for becoming an attraction for people.

If we're honest and sincere to ourselves, we will establish trust and build credibility with other people.

In boosting self-confidence by gaining confidence in ourselves, we are able to attract people attracted by our positivity and charm.

In embracing these characteristics by embracing these qualities, we will be able to build solid lasting relationships, and ultimately become an influential force around the globe.

Tips For Improving Your Communication Skills

Enhancing your communication skills could transform the way you conduct your life at work and in your personal life.

You may be looking to develop more relationships, grow your career or communicate more effectively There are a variety of easy and effective methods to increase your communications skills.

Here are some suggestions which have been helpful to me:

Active listening is when you listen attentively, you demonstrate to others that we are interested about what they've got have to say. Try listening with no interruptions by asking questions that clarify the meaning of what's being discussed, and writing down what you've learned to demonstrate that you've absorbed.

Keep it simple and clear: In all communications with others, we must be condensed and simple. Do not use jargons or confusing language. Attempt to convey your message using a clear and simple language.

Utilize nonverbal communications: Nonverbal communications, like your body language, and the tone of your voice, could be a significant influence on the way others view us. Utilize a clear expressions, keep eye contact and employ an amiable tone of voice that conveys the warmth and the feeling of openness.

Get feedback from your family, friends, or your colleagues to provide comments on your skills in communicating. This will help you pinpoint the areas you could develop and improve your confidence.

Training, practicing, and practice As with any ability, communicating requires practicing. Find opportunities to improve your skills in communication for example, giving presentations at work, or engaging in discussions with strangers.

Find out about communication classes If you're having trouble in your communications look into expert coaching or training. You'll get individual feedback and assistance in order to assist you in improving your communication skills.

Keep learning Communication is a complicated ability, with always room to improve. Learn as much as you can and testing new strategies Be willing to fail.

Enhancing your communication skills may be a long-term process that requires time and energy, but the results are worth it.

When you become more proficient at communicating You can develop stronger relations, attain greater results in your professional life and be able to express yourself better.

Chapter 10: Building Strong Connections

Maintaining strong connections and building connections is vital to your professional and personal well-being.

In our fast-paced society It's easy to become distracted by our personal life and lose sight of the significance of our human connection.

There are many reasons keeping and building relations is vital:

The emotional support of strong connections can offer us emotional assistance during tough times. If you're facing an emotional time and need somebody to talk with and confide in can help a lot. Through building relationships that are strong that we have built, we'll be able to create the foundation for a network of support that will aid us through the challenges and ups.

The process of building relationships through networking are also beneficial to the professional life. When we network and make connections, we create many opportunities to advance our career. If it's locating a new job or receiving recommendations for promotions solid relationships will help you advance in your career.

More effective communication: When you have strong relationships it's easier to be able to effectively communicate with other people. We can understand the perspectives of each other and speak with respect and effective. This will result in higher levels of positive interaction and greater results.

Happier: Research has revealed that healthy relationships can be a major factor in our general happiness and wellbeing. Through the development and maintenance of good relationships, it is possible to boost our contentment and happiness.

Feeling of belonging: Building connections can create a sense of belonging as well as a sense of sense of community. When we've got a strong social network, it makes us feel as if we are part of something larger beyond ourselves. It can give us the feeling of belonging and satisfaction.

The bottom line is that building solid connections and keeping them is crucial to the well-being of our professional and personal lives.

It could be emotional support or networking, improved communications, greater happiness or feeling of belonging the importance of relationships is a major aspect of our life.

Therefore, take time to develop and keep solid relationships with the people who are around you. This is an investment in the well-being of yourself and your family and is worth it.

How To Actively Listen And Show Empathy

Being able to listen and show empathy are crucial skills that help enhance our communication and relationships with other people.

Here are some helpful tips for how you can actively listen and display empathy

Concentrate on the conversation If someone is talking and you are listening, be sure to give them all your focus. That means turning off your mobile phone, shutting off the television, and paying attention only on the speaker. When you do this, it will demonstrate that you appreciate and admire the person as well as the words they are sharing.

Display interest: Let the other person you're curious about the things they've got to say through asking open-ended questions, and encouraging them to share their feelings and thoughts. They will be heard and feel understood.

Reflect on to what someone else has spoken to prove you are able to comprehend and attentive. You can do this through a summary of what the person has said by paraphrasing the words they've spoken or just nodding employing verbal signals to demonstrate that you've been listening.

Engage in empathy. Empathy is placing yourself in another's position and understanding their point of view. Be compassionate by acknowledging person's feelings, and expressing an the empathy they're experiencing.

Be respectful: interrupting someone may be rude and cause problems with communication. Give the person time to complete what they're saying prior to speaking up.

Do not judge: Try to avoid judging the individual or their opinions and emotions. Instead, you should approach conversations with an open mind, and an eagerness to learn.

Utilize body language. Use your body language to indicate that you're listening actively and engaged with the conversation. You can do this by keeping the eye's contact and nodding as well as using facial expressions to demonstrate interest and understanding.

Through active listening and showing compassion, we are able to improve the relationships we have with people around us and strengthen our connections.

The skills are applicable to any circumstance, whether you're having a conversation with a friend or an official gathering.

If you're ever in conversations with someone else you know, put these ideas into practice and then see how it enhances your connection and communication to others.

The Power of Giving Back and Showing Appreciation

Being grateful and showing gratitude are powerful actions that boost our connections and general health.

Below are some of the main reasons:

Feeling of sense of purpose: Volunteering gives us an inner sense of meaning and satisfaction. In helping other people, it feels like you're having a positive effect on the world. We are making a difference that is greater than us. It can boost our sense of satisfaction and happiness our lives.

Increased relations If we express gratitude and respect to one another in our lives, we build stronger relationships with those around us. When we acknowledge their contribution and acknowledging their contributions and appreciation, we demonstrate our appreciation and love for their contributions. This could result in greater positive interactions as well as deeper bonds.

Greater empathy: Being kind and showing gratitude could also improve the empathy of other people. In putting ourselves in who is not like us and looking at the world as they see it and perspective, we will develop an increased sense of compassion and empathy.

A positive impact on other people giving back and showing gratitude can create positive effects on people. In helping those who is in need, or showing gratitude for their efforts to the community, we have the potential to have a profound impact on their lives and increase the quality of their life.

Increased self-esteem by giving gratitude and expressing appreciation could increase our self-esteem and confidence in ourselves. When we contribute to something greater than ourselves, and acknowledging other's contributions, you feel a higher sense of meaning and worth within our lives.

As a result, giving to others and showing gratitude are powerful actions that boost our relationships, overall well-being as well as overall satisfaction.

In helping those around us, showing gratitude and appreciating the efforts of others it is possible to have an positive difference in the world as well as strengthen our bonds with the people in our lives.

If you ever have the chance to help others or show your appreciation, make sure you do the time to do it. This is an investment in your personal well-being as well as the wellbeing of people who are around you.

Chapter 11: Networking Strategies

Networking is a crucial aspect to a professional career.

Here are some suggestions for creating the foundation for a successful professional network.

Participate in social events, industry-related meetings, and seminars to connect with professionals in the field you work in. This is an excellent occasion to meet new people and gain insight into industry trends and the best methods.

Utilize social media social media websites such as LinkedIn for connecting with other experts in your field. Join professional organizations and engage in discussion forums to increase your online presence as well as expand your networks.

Introduce yourself: Ask your network members for introductions to professionals in your field. This is a fantastic method to make new friends as well as expand your network.

Take initiative: Reach out to those whom you admire, or have a job or a company you are keen on. You can send them an email or a text message an email, and then introduce yourself. Make it clear your motives for reaching out as well as the benefits you're hoping to get by the relationship.

Follow-up: Once you have met an acquaintance for the first time, ensure to keep in touch with the person. Write a thank-you email or text message, and stay on contact in order to develop an ongoing relationship.

Provide value when networking consider ways you could be of something of value to other people. Give your experience and knowledge and offer to link to others within your circle, or offer the resources and assistance.

Do your best to be yourself in your networking activities and when building connections. Being authentic is essential to build relationships and trust with other people.

Be patient. Building solid networks takes patience and time. Do not expect immediately results. However, be constant in your efforts and work to build your network.

If you follow these guidelines by following these suggestions, you will be able to build strong connections with your professional contacts and create new opportunities for your professional development.

How to Make a lasting Impressions and Stand Out in the Crowd Making an lasting impression, and standing out in the crowd can be difficult particularly in the current rapidly-moving and highly competitive environment. But, there are many methods that will help you create a lasting impression, and stand out the rest of the crowd.

Genuineness is the key to creating an impact. Stay true to who you are and let your character and distinctive qualities be evident. It will help you reach out to others at a deeper level, and help you stand out in the rest of the pack.

Be stylish and professional: Dressing properly and professionally to your event will assist you in making a good impression. Be sure that your attire will fit well, is neat and tidy, as well as suitable for the occasion or venue.

Be positive Positive attitude and energy will help you make yourself stand out. Be friendly, smile and demonstrate an interest in people. It will help you create a good impressions and create lasting relations.

Have confidence: Being confident is beautiful and helps to stand out from the crowd. Make eye contact, and communicate with confidence and clarity. It will help you get the attention of others and make yourself memorable.

Tell your story Share your story. Sharing your personal stories and personal experiences is a great way to leave an impact on others. Make yourself vulnerable and real and tell what makes you different and intriguing.

Prepare yourself: Being well-prepared and well-informed can allow you to make a mark in the crowd. Be thorough, aware of current happenings, and be prepared with relevant inquiries and tips.

Make yourself memorable: Discover ways to stand out, be it through a memorable business card, memorable exchange, or an exceptional ability or talent. Find methods to highlight your talents and distinctive qualities.

If you follow these tips using these tips, you'll be able to create an impact and stand out from an crowded.

Always be genuine and confident, uplifting and ready You can find ways to stand out and show off your distinctive qualities.

With just a little work and imagination, you will create a lasting impression and be noticed regardless of the setting.

The Importance of Follow-up And Staying in Touch

The process of networking and building relationships is just a small part of the fight.

Another part is keeping the relationships you've made and staying connected to the people who you've gotten to know.

Staying connected is essential to creating lasting, strong relationships as well as opening possibilities in your life as well as professional.

The first step towards staying in contact is to contact you following your first meeting or exchange.

It could be as easy as sending an mail or message to say thank you the person for their time and to express your commitment to keeping in touch.

If it's appropriate, you could even suggest a event or collaboration.

After establishing a relationship and established a connection, you must stay connected frequently.

This could be as easy as sending an message or email to keep track of how the people are doing.

Additionally, you can share material or articles that may appeal to your readers or invite them for meetings or events.

Social media are also an effective tool to stay connected.

Join LinkedIn and other platforms, and follow their latest posts and news.

This will help you stay on top of your game and help you keep in touch.

It is important to make keeping in contact a routine schedule.

Make reminders, or schedule periodic check-ins so that you aren't letting too long slip by without calling for help.

As you keep connected, the stronger the relationship you will have and the greater opportunities that will open up.

As well as strengthening connections, keeping in contact could also lead to many new possibilities.

Some of your connections may have the ability to introduce you to people you haven't met before or provide some new possibilities, but only if your name is at their radar, and continue to maintain the connection.

In the end, keeping in touch will show how much you appreciate the friendship and cherish people you've made contact with.

Through following up, remaining connected, and consistently communicating with your contacts to build solid and lasting connections that could help you in a variety of ways.

As a result, keeping in touch and keeping in contact with your contacts is vital to establish durable, lasting relationships and in securing new possibilities in your own professional lives.

Make it an habit and then use social media for your benefit.

Make it clear that you appreciate the connection and love those you've met And you'll be able to reap advantages in the longer term.

Chapter 12: Overcoming Social Anxiety

A social anxiety disorder is prevalent problem that affects a large number of individuals, and has a major effect on the way they establish and keep friendships.

Social anxiety is a form of anxiety disorder defined by the constant fear of social settings and negative opinions from others.

Social anxiety sufferers are likely to avoid social interactions completely They may also experience an intense fear when engaged in social settings.

The stress of social anxiety may have significant effects on relationships since it makes it more difficult for individuals to start new connections and to maintain their current ones.

Individuals with anxiety about social interaction might be reluctant to meet strangers or take part in activities with others and this can reduce the opportunities to make friends.

Additionally, they may be unable to keep relationships going because of fear of being rejected or negative judgement, which may cause feelings of loneliness and isolation.

Alongside the effect on the way relationships are formed and maintained stress and anxiety in social relationships can influence the level of the relationships.

Individuals with anxiety about social interaction can have difficulty speaking out or effectively communicating, which may lead to confusion as well as conflicts within relations.

Additionally, they may be unable to participate alongside their spouse or partake at social gatherings and events, which may reduce their social experiences as well as create feelings of isolation.

If you're suffering from issues with social anxiety and are struggling to maintain relationship issues, it's crucial to seek help and therapy.

Cognitive behavioral therapy (CBT) is a successful treatment for anxiety about social situations, because it teaches people to recognize and confront the negative beliefs and thoughts regarding social interactions.

The use of medication can also help to manage the symptoms of social anxiety.

As well as seeking help There are other actions you can adopt to alleviate social anxiety and strengthen your social relationships.

You can, for instance, begin with relaxation exercises like deep breathing, or gradual muscle relaxation in order to alleviate anxiety and stress when you are in social settings.

Also, you can develop your skills in communication including assertiveness and active listening for helping you better navigate situations in social settings.

Social anxiety may affect relationships. However, it's a condition that can be treated.

In seeking out help or treatment and gaining techniques to reduce anxiety as well as improve communication, you'll be better able to maintain and build positive relationships.

Tips For Overcoming Social Anxiety And Building Confidence in Social Situations

Social anxiety is difficult to deal to, however there are a variety of methods that will help you get over your fear and increase confidence when it comes to social interactions.

Negative thoughts can be challenged:

Social anxiety can be caused by the negative attitudes and thoughts about self and the social environment.

When you question these beliefs and ideas, you'll be able to start to see them in a an optimistic light.

If, for instance, you think of "everyone is judging me," question the thought by determining whether there's any evidence to back up that idea.

In most cases you'll find this notion is not grounded upon actual reality.

Practice relaxation techniques:

The stress of anxiety can cause physical symptoms like a fast heartbeat, sweating, breathing problems.

Engaging in relaxation methods such as deep breathing, gradual muscle relaxation and meditation could aid in reducing physical discomfort and make you feel more relaxed and more relaxed when you are in social settings.

Start with a small amount:

If you're feeling overwhelmed by social interactions begin with small-scale goals you can set to you.

As an example, you might begin by greeting your coworker, or attend an informal social event with acquaintances you've met.

When you're more at ease in these situations You can slowly move to more difficult scenarios.

Concentrate on the other person:

Instead of being focused on your own anxieties and self-doubt, concentrate on others.

Be curious and ask questions. to what other people are saying. It can make you feel more connected with people around you and feel less self-conscious.

Ask for help:

It may be beneficial seeking help from a therapist, or a help group.

Therapists can assist you to create strategies for coping and help you tackle any issues which could be causing your anxiety about social interactions.

Support groups can give you a the feeling of belonging and connection to others that are experiencing similar situations.

Practice social skills:

Social skills training can make to feel more comfortable when it comes to social interactions.

Practice skills including making small talk as well as active listening and assertiveness.

Playing role-playing with friends or a relatives member is an effective way of practicing the skills you need to master in a secure and loving setting.

Be proud of your achievements:

Be proud of your accomplishments and recognize them regardless of how insignificant they might seem.

Each time you confront your fears and leap out of your home, you're working towards conquering the social anxiety that you have and gaining confidence in social settings.

Beating social anxiety and gaining confidence in social settings is a process that requires patience and time.

However, with the correct techniques and the right support the right strategies and support, you will be able to build the confidence and skills that you require to be more at ease and secure when socializing.

The Importance of Taking Small Steps And Setting Achievable Goals

When it comes to reaching the goals we set it's easy to become focused on the larger image and forget about our small steps to complete to reach our goals.

Setting achievable targets and taking baby actions is essential for the success of our lives, both professionally and personally.

First, setting realistic objectives and then taking small steps can help us stay away from becoming overwhelmed.

When we concentrate on the bigger picture, it is often difficult to determine what to do as well as feeling like the aim is not achievable.

But breaking down the ultimate goal into manageable, smaller steps helps us concentrate on each step separately and progress toward our goal without becoming overwhelmed.

Second, setting realistic goals by taking small steps can help in building confidence.

If we accomplish small objectives in the process It creates a sense of satisfaction and inspires us to push ahead.

It builds confidence in us and helps us tackle more challenging challenges in the future.

A third point is taking small steps, and reaching small-scale objectives allows us to change our direction as required.

If we establish a large target and solely focus on it, without taking tiny steps on the way and we don't realize until we're too late to realize we're heading in that direction in the wrong way.

When we set achievable targets and taking incremental steps to achieve them, we are able to reassess the progress we have made and alter our plan in order to ensure that we're in the right direction towards achieving our ultimate goal.

In the end, making tiny steps and working towards smaller goals can help us gain momentum.

Each time we reach a small objective, we increase our momentum toward our objective, making it more simple to continue moving towards our ultimate goal.

This energy can be very strong and could allow us to accomplish things that you never imagined possible.

As a summary, taking the smallest steps to set achievable targets is crucial to the success of our lives as a professional and personally.

Chapter 13: Navigating Difficult Relationships

Being able to maintain positive relationships with people isn't always simple sometimes; it is possible to be with difficult or even challenging relationship.

It's also important to be aware that how we respond to these scenarios can dramatically affect the results of the relationship, as well as our personal well-being and mental wellbeing.

It is crucial to be able to approach relationships that are difficult in a positive way.

Focusing on the positives of your relationship, and willingness to tackle any issues that may arise.

Also, it is important to maintain an attitude of optimism and a sense of hope in the direction of the partnership.

Second, it's crucial to be honest and open to the person you are communicating with.

It is about expressing what we feel in a positive and positive manner. It also means still being open to other people's perspectives.

Communication is essential in maintaining and building strong relationships even in challenging situations.

The third thing to remember is that you must define boundaries and follow the boundaries.

This is about defining what we'll and will not allow in our relationships and expressing these rules to each other.

When we establish and enforce boundaries, we will be able to shield ourselves from being abused of or abused in relationships.

Fourthly, it's essential to work on forgiveness and let loose of any anger.

The stoic or bitterness we hold toward the person you disagree with is harmful and can hinder the relationship from progressing in our relationship.

When we practice forgiveness it is possible to let go of the negative feelings and make an environment for growth and healing in our relationships.

In the end, it's crucial to put self-care first and self-care and mental wellbeing.

It means that we take the time to take care of ourselves physically emotionally and mentally without sacrificing our personal well-being for the difficulties in a relation.

When we prioritize our desires, we are able to enter the situation with a more clear thinking and more positive mindset.

The bottom line is that managing difficult relationships while maintaining an optimistic attitude is difficult, however it's essential to approach difficult situations by embracing optimism, open and honest lines of communication, clear boundaries forgiveness and self-care.

When we do this it is possible to work toward creating and maintaining connections that enrich us as well as bring happiness and satisfaction.

Tips For Dealing With Conflict And Resolving Disagreements

Conflict is a necessary aspect of relationships no matter if it's business or personal.

How we manage conflict will greatly affect the outcomes of a disagreement and also the general health of our relationship.

Here are some suggestions for solving conflict and for differences:

Be prepared to face the situation by keeping an open mind It's crucial to view the problem with an open-minded mind without preconceived notions or assumptions. Be sure to consider the viewpoint of another person and consider their perspective prior to jumping to conclusions or taking a position based on assumptions.

Keep your focus on the topic that is at hand: Focus only on the particular issue which is the cause of conflict and refrain from bringing up previous concerns or topics unrelated to the current one. This helps to keep the discussion focused and effective.

Utilize "I" statements: Use "I" statements instead of "you" statements when expressing what you're feeling. In other words rather than saying "You always make me feel ignored," use the phrase "I feel ignored when I don't get a response to my messages." This strategy can stop someone else from getting defensive, and keep conversations positive.

Don't blame or attack Don't blame or attack someone else during the discussion. Instead, you should focus on the problem in hand and work in finding the best solution for both sides.

If you're in need of a break, take it In the event that a conversation gets excessively heated or uncontrollable, it's fine to break the conversation and then return in the future. This will help to prevent an argument from getting out of hand and let both parties engage in the discussion with an open mind.

Seek common ground Look for an area where there is agreement that you can build upon. This helps to establish the sense of teamwork as well as cooperation, which can help you find an answer that is beneficial to both sides.

If you require help, seek outside assistance If the dispute can't be resolved by both parties, you should seek external assistance from a counselor or mediator. An impartial third party could offer a new perspective and assist in facilitating a positive discussion.

The bottom line is that dealing with conflicts and working out disagreements demands an open-minded mind with clear communication as well as an ability to work in finding an acceptable solution for all parties. Focusing on the problem that is at hand, not blaming or blame, and looking for an agreement, we are able to solve conflict in a constructive and constructive manner.

The Importance of Setting Boundaries And Staying True to Yourself

The ability to set boundaries and remain in your own truth is vital to maintain healthy relationships as well as a sense of confidence.

These are the reasons:

Insuring your emotional and mental wellbeing:

Set boundaries to protect your mental and emotional well-being by setting limits to the things you will allow others to do.

With boundaries set By setting limits, you'll be able to stay clear of situations that cause you to feel unsafe or uncomfortable and ensure your well-being is prioritized.

Maintaining healthy relationships

Boundaries are used to establish what is expected and the responsibilities of every person involved in a partnership, whether that's either professional or personal.

This will help avoid misunderstandings or conflicts and help result in a more positive and mutually beneficial dynamic.

Empowering self-respect

In setting limits, you're telling others that your values and needs are essential and must be acknowledged.

It can also help to build confidence in oneself and build self-esteem. This will in turn create greater positive interactions and relationships with other people.

Avoiding burnout:

Set boundaries will also aid in preventing burnout by making sure that you do not take on too much responsibility, or sacrifice yourself in order to benefit other people.

When you establish limits for your time and energy you'll be able to keep a good balanced work/life life, and prevent exhaustion or even resentment.

Keep your commitment to yourself.

The setting of boundaries will allow you to stay loyal to your principles and values instead of conforming to the demands or expectations of other people.

It can create confidence and trust in interactions with people in addition to a more solid feeling of your own persona.

When creating boundaries, it's crucial to clearly communicate these boundaries and in a respectful manner to those around you.

This could mean setting limitations regarding your availability or time or establishing rules for your behaviour or communication as well as simply declaring "no" when something doesn't coincide with your beliefs or your priorities.

Also, it is important to remain constant in the way you enforce your limits and to communicate any modifications when needed.

Chapter 14: Highlight Your Alluring Characteristics

Remember when you were in an elevated state of mind and one in some way or other, everyone seemed to be responding to your thoughts. The people were more attentive and more interested, but somehow captivated by your.

It's not uncommon to experience these moments maybe you were awake at the top of the bed or had a optimistic mood that day. They are fleeting but they echo in your memory with incredible power. It's hard to find a better feeling than knowing that people are truly and distinctly affected by our actions.

Take a moment to think back on those days. What were the qualities of you that enticed people? What traits were encased your personality? Do you believe that you entertained more than you expected? Are you more energetic? Did you listen more?

The attractiveness of someone can be everything. Certain people can be enticing and make others be able to relax quickly. They are usually light playful, while others are drawn by their vivacious passion. Certain models are a bit puzzling and hard to read and draw other people by generating fascination, but I'm only naming some examples.

The characteristics of each person differ from one to another and it doesn't matter if the person's attractiveness is similar to someone else's. Think of someone you know as entertaining and with humor as their most appealing aspect. Are their jokes the identical to that of others? If somebody else in your life has copied their style, would that imitator's style be just similar to the original?

Everyone's appealing qualities are unique to each person. No one smiles the same as you do. No one is captivating or entertaining in the similar way to you. In this way, we're not doing well in the event that we try to imitate the charm of another.

When I was younger I was well-known for sporting a self-deprecating smile. I realized that I could make some pretty racy or bold remarks when I swung with a smile along whatever I said, and it was evident that this would be a requirement for me to have an exaggeration style. (but I didn't do this deliberately).

My wonderful companion at that moment, let's call him Mike is currently observing appealing characteristics. After we had a chat, Mike started (unknowingly) making a joke about himself in order to play the role of a teaser, just like that I had. But the problem was that it wasn't the way he was accustomed to. Mike's smile was not deemed unnatural and he was able to do a better job than the way I did regardless, and his words were basically identical. My style wasn't the same for Mike.

Mike has lived in several countries lived in various cultures, and spoke in five languages. Mike found that his experiences as well as his education attracted those who he was most drawn to, as he emphasized this particular aspect of himself, aside from being more attractive to women, he also found that there were more girls interested in the other women, but more people were attracted to him in general. It was difficult for me to bring the same qualities as he did to attract people since the quality was not present in my own.

Consider which of your personal traits attracted the majority of people before, your strengths that other people seem to gravitate toward. Have you ever been applauded for? Have people been impressed by your work? Incredibly attracted by your work?

You might be charming, funny, or even energetic. Your smile could light up an entire room, or you're such a pleasant person that people can't resist the desire to be attracted by your.

Find this trait in your own self and actively work to highlight it.

Take it up to the in front of you. This may seem as a form of self-focus, but the truth is that knowing that oneself is among the greatest types of data.

If you highlight your finest qualities, you'll radiate a unique charm that is truly distinctive for you. This is what will draw people to you.

Like any ad agency will inform you, it's a lot better to attract people rather than pursue them.

Individual Concentration

There is nothing that are more appealing or tempting than when a person you love needs to know you personally. They must know what's most important to you, the person is at the center of your being as well as your desires, thoughts, your emotions, or your fears anxiety.

They'd rather not be able to identify the truth about you, for no reasons that they have. They're making a conscious effort to discover problems or weaknesses that they can't control. They're obligated to be aware of that they're so strongly attracted to you, they don't have any control over their own behavior.

They must be aware of you because you're unique. type, and the more people get to know you, how they interact with them from.

Such encounters are extremely rarely in everyday life. In the moment we truly appreciate them with their beauty, they carry huge value and are so rare, it's impossible not to be enthralled by them, and then be sucked into the awe of them.

Most people revolve about their own needs. What do they require to know, their desires, how they can satisfy themselves. People often say in discussions to be attentive and trust that the other person will speak. The problem is that they don't understand, but they do are focused on answering. There is a good chance that we may in some way to blame because, in the end humans have an nature to be able to look after the first priority.

But, if someone feels so strongly attracted to us, and they want to get to know us, and only our names, and when they remember every single detail about our personalities, and all of our habits, it's incredibly challenging to avoid being attracted by them.

In the event we decide to change the table in the event that we can apply this concept to the person we really want and if we present them with a unique centre that is unique to them and only them, we smudge a bit of their individuality and they will not resist from doing it.

Their Vanity.

The one that is adored by everyone Is "Me". It doesn't matter if they claim they'd rather not discuss their own lives, or whether you tell people that you could talk about ourselves.

The moment when someone truly is tuning in and truly spending the time and effort to understand us, since they want to understand us. they're listening without judgment and listening to understand.

All people need to be seen. If you are willing to take time to understand the other person, you'll eventually become a key person in their life.

Additionally, we must be noticed. It is important to pay and observed. The main focus of individual examination will focus on the two various ways if there is enough opportunity and attention from the other side prior to all else.

It's one of the main characters in the guideline for correspondence. When you're given a huge amount of attention and insight and consideration,.

Chapter 15: Secret

The secret is at the heart of attraction.

Actually, along with real friendship there is a desire for individual interaction and satisfaction of individual desire.

The thrill of being able to know someone else starts with an attraction - there's no connection with them, yet you're captivated by them and it drives the desire to find out more.

Then there's the excitement and almost gentle anticipation of how they react. Do they react to you? There are signs that they might be getting drawn towards the person you are. They stare at you for just a moment longer than they should while you are cooperating with them. Your bodies do not exceed the boundaries of each other's personal space. You can't guarantee in the event they love you no matter how they like you, or in a similar way.

They keep their secrets to prevent you from speculating.

Being able to meet someone else is possibly the most amazing things in every day life. It is a source of fascination, with the to-and-fro/drift in and out between you could be considered fascinating and locks you into. If you have met someone whom that you liked then they immediately shared their feelings to let you know about that they love you to death while you do not have met them and it removes a good amount of the nonsense out of your communication.

It is clear where they stand and you know the position they take. It takes away the feeling of vulnerability and takes away a good part of the excitement and the rush of interest and allowing you to continue to get to know their personalities.

This eliminates the never-ending curiosity that is beginning any interest.

In the present, I know that there are people who will be able to comprehend this and respond:

However, it is exactly how you should conduct yourself as you must remain clear and honest in your opinions and don't need to play around.

..what's most important, I can hear that you. However, there are not a lot of us that are completely inaccessible to the snub of. It is true that weakness can be a source of ridicule which is why, in the event that you say to someone that you love them it is putting your name out there, and putting the entire power of the hands of that person. They are the sole decision-maker. Then they can decide whether to stay or leave in the event that the position you are in is incredibly evident.

You're not revealing your personal information too quick, speaking less frequently and whenever you do speak, by introducing yourself with some interest, and a hint to keep them in curiosity and have them speculate. You know you love you, they sense that from your non-verbal communications and voice, but there's no way to prove it and they aren't 100 % certain.

It's keeping track of your curiosity, and that is why you need to keep in touch with your personal secrets.

Maintaining a secretive lifestyle is a simple thing to perform. When you're focusing on someone, as you're giving them individual attention maintaining a secrets is easy since you'll want to know what they are up to. Giving someone the ability to speak about their own life typically means that they'll be less revealing about themselves.

Beware of the urge to ramble on about your opinions on what someone else says. When you offer something that's close to your hearts, be wary of the desire to respond with "Ok, I'm with you and now let me explain what I believe'. Let them talk.

You'll be able to keep the attention of your admirers and will continue to keep their fascination for your character.

The same is true for the underlying stages of collaboration. If you're more comfortable with someone it is normal to talk details about yourself. However, as the relationship was continuous, attraction will surely have grown greater than when you put it all open before anything other things (it may not even reached the point of reassurance to the extent that you didn't).

It's not that I'm saying it's wrong to not share anything concerning yourself throughout the duration of your relationship with someone. However, relationships don't really work in this way.

The only thing I'm suggesting is to concentrate on the person undoubtedly more as you get familiar with the person. Beware of the desire to speak about yourself in a way that is too revealing and just pay attentively to the person you are getting to know to understand the person. In this way, you'll be able to remain in the loop about your secrets that will keep their interest in you.

Chapter 16: Want

That's probably the primary issue. But not their craving, it's yours. Your desire will unify everything.

If you are truly in need of your own, personal focus and focusing on your saga is simple.

It's more than that simple, in fact. In the event that you are truly looking for a single and get to know the person on an intimate personal level will be most simple in the world, because for there is nothing else you have to accomplish.

It's crucial to feel a genuine desire driving you. This doesn't mean just the most heartfelt of cravings, but I'm referring to every craving, to you as well as to others.

If you want to live a truly satisfied life, you have to desire it to the point of going through the agony of growth. If you're aspire to learn more about this intriguing outsider who is at the station, your desire should be strong enough to overcome the fear of rejection. The desire is the primary motivation for everything you decide to do. Without it, you'll be like an automobile trying to operate with a tank that isn't fully filled.

In terms of human attraction Your desire for another person is not valid unless it's documented. In other words, your love is in their individuality rather than for the benefits you might get from them.

The woman in the corner could be stunning, which is obviously a major factor to what attracts anyone but after some conversations are you drawn to her because of her uniqueness or because of her appearance? Do you find her character to be a magnet for your attention or do you just want to be to her? Someone you've been keeping an interest in is interesting but also shrewd, and stable financially. Would you like him to be who he is because the guy is a good long-term accomplice in the surface?

It is a stark contrast between wanting to have to be a person for yourself and lusting after them for the things you could gain from them is an example of self-centeredness. Our species is incredibly complex and by advances in technology, we've created the ability to recognize skill.

We are able to recognize when someone just wants us to help them with what they will receive from us. This is especially a reason to be frightened as nobody wants to feel they're paying attention to consideration as a necessity.

This is similar to when salesmen come up to you in the middle of the night. They care nothing about you and are only looking to make an offer, which is why there are many who have certain resentment towards them because of their childish zeal.

Similar to the case that you sense a person paying attention to you because the person wants to sleep to you. Or however in the event that you sense a woman putting her energy into you because she wants to give her is the most tangible thing you could offer.

These two scenarios make a bad impression on the individual we are judging. In the event that we are doing identical things to someone else when we only want what we will receive from them, chances will be that they'll notice our low-mindedness and will be viewed as untruthful, manipulative and even angry.

In the event that you feel an individual as a person who is appealing to you Consider where the desire originates and what it is driving you. Does your desire at any moment be fulfilled with the help of that person? On the other hand, can anyone do it?

In the event that this is the only option available and you're not interested in to be with someone who isn't a good fit for the reason that you don't know what they're about. Perhaps you should let them go, and allow them to locate someone else willing to help them and discover someone who ignites an actual fire in you.

In the event you do not like them as the person they truly are, getting to understand who they are really are is a challenge. The person will present an appearance of not being trustworthy or even manipulative. people around you will recognize the fake.

You'll be driven by your desire to. Make sure it's facing outwards, and not towards the inside.

Remember when people were positively influenced by you. find out what attracted them. Then, bring out that element in your own. People are likely to be drawn by you when you're highlighting the best qualities of you, because you'll radiate a distinctive personality that's one of one of a kind for you and only the two of you.

Focus on their distinctiveness. Learn to understand them as what they really are. Your focus should be to the outside, and rather than inward towards you.

You should usually keep track of the latest developments in your life and keep them interested by narrowing down their interests rather than putting it all immediately.

Three things that will draw you any person you'd like. However, the intensity of your desires will determine which you'll need to draw.

Be sure that your passion is focused on that person you're interested in and not what you might gain from the person. You are driven by your desire, it's like your sense of direction. Be in tune with your instincts and it will lead you to the person you truly require, and who you really connect with.

In this way, you'll be able to attract anyone you want but you don't need to because of the fact that you'll get drawn to the people you truly would like to be.

You can ask this question in 3 words. The primary question you may ask your friends is , 'How do you feel doing?' However, you should really ask this question and really pay on the responses. We are so molded to involving this as a hello as opposed to an inquiry the words have lost their significance so attempt to track down alternate approaches to asking like, 'What's been happening in your life/world/work/family and so forth' or ask particulars like 'How are your youngsters?' Which is your spouse and the list goes on. The one I have is my GP typically asks two times He asks "how are you" I reply, 'I'm fine I'm fine', and he replies "OK, do you know how? If he repeats the question, usually gets a better response.

Chapter 17: Consider Your Fellowships a Speculation

The feeling of being connected and kinship are just as important for a healthy lifestyle just as exercise and diet are therefore; you need to take care of it similarly. As if you had thought you were healthy, your body would soon blur should you aren't aware of your relationships, you will also see them blur. Be sure to keep track of your acquaintances and keep an eye on the future. It's an incredible way to stay informed of events within a person's life; however it's an inactive gadget. There is nothing that can strengthen friendships more than connecting with one another ... although perhaps being out of the mindset, but via the phone or Skype, Face Time or comparable.

Ask questions about pressing questions and be attentive to responses

The best way to interact with people is to seek clarification regarding pressing questions and then take note of your responses. Most people are terrible people to be around and waiting to get an opportunity to share their thoughts and, therefore, if you can prove that you're able to pay attention for what someone needs to share and build your conversation around their responses, there is a much greater likelihood of creating a reputable connection. Pay attention, stay until the conversation is over before proceeding in your query, and then focus the information they've given you and find out more on it more in depth. Signs that are not verbal, such as gesturing or smiling or making a sound of listening, such as 'ah huh", "gee" and using phrases such as 'truly', "go to', and "let me know" are essential.

Tell us about your experiences

When listening is the effective way to create a solid relationship with someone it is important to open up and talk about your own life also. Kinships can be based on similarity and common traits, which is why you should be open about your own. Just make sure that you're not exaggerating and limit your exchanges between you to a minimum of 50% the time.

Provide gratifying and genuine praise

Make sure you praise them in ways that show that you're similar to them. Do not just declare 'that's a nice skirt'. Instead, you should say "I love your dress.' If you are required to look like an obnoxious stalker or a character from the movie Single White Female you want to be sure that you're focused on the real resemblances and also that your compliments can be verified. There is nothing that can turn off potential partners faster than a fake.

Be genuine

If you're looking to attract new acquaintances, look for common interests with them practically and trigger them to be aware of your regular interactions. When you are in a conversation, use phrases such as 'I can understand what you're trying to say and

'I thought so often "I understand it," etc. which show you're at a common frequency. Engage in a positive way, open and enthusiastic, focus on your positive attitude, smile and keep going like a person that truly enjoys the world around them.

Concentrate on your non-verbal communication Smile and keep it up

Smiles are everything. It conveys a variety of factors - it conveys love as well as interest, and it also shows transparency. Also, it says a good amount about you. It reveals that you're happy in your life, you're drawing people into the scene and are an individual who would like to have close. Make a smile and gestures when someone is speaking. Be aware of your non-verbal communication. Keep your stance open and keep your arms straight. Take note of the space of the other person's space, but should you the appropriate time comes to touch the shoulder or lower part of their body in order to establish a connection.

The word "attractive" doesn't refer to looking great and wearing a well-made outfit or being professional. The most important things people love aren't items they can see at first. Being fascinated means taking pride in yourself, displaying your confidence as well as being attentive to others as well as being completely free of such as to keep yourself from self-pity and massive pleasure. If you're trying to discover how you can attract others' attention and discover the ideal methods of attracting the people around you, take a look now!

www.ingramcontent.com/pod-product-compliance
Lightning Source LLC
Chambersburg PA
CBHW071445080526
44587CB00014B/2001